David Curwen

NARROW GAUGE RAILWAY SOCIETY

Serving the narrow gauge world since 1951

MEMBERSHIP SECRETARY : Lawson Little, 1 Archers Drive, Old Bilsthorpe, Newark, Notts. NG22 8SD
TREASURER : Ron Allison, 21A Spring Lane, Balderton, Newark, NG24 3NZ

The Society was founded in 1951 to encourage interest in all forms of narrow gauge rail transport. Members' interests cover every aspect of the construction, operation, history and modelling of narrow gauge railways throughout the world. Society members receive this magazine and Narrow Gauge News, a bi-monthly review of current events on the narrow gauge scene. An extensive library, locomotive record and modelling information service are available to members. Meetings are arranged by local groups based in Leeds, Lincoln, London, Malvern and Stoke-on-Trent. Annual subscription currently £18, due April 1st.

THE NARROW GAUGE

ISBN 978-0-9554326-1-3
ISSN 0142-5587

EDITOR : Alan Burgess, 6 The Crescent, Orton Longueville, Peterborough PE2 7DT
Email : aamarketing@btconnect.com
BACK NUMBER SALES : Lawson Little, 1 Archers Drive, Old Bilsthorpe, Newark, Notts. NG22 8SD

Price £9.95 when bought **Issue 202**

Published by the Narrow Gauge Railway Society to record the history and development of narrow gauge rail transport. Our intention is to present a well balanced, well-illustrated publication, and the editor welcomes original articles, photographs and drawings for consideration. Articles should preferably be submitted as Word files by e-mail, otherwise written or typed with double spacing on one side of the paper only. Conventional photographs generally still provide better reproduction quality than images sent by e-mail or on CD ROM. The editor appreciates a stamped addressed envelope if a reply or return of material is required. A range of back numbers is available from the address above.

AUTHOR'S NOTE

Whilst every effort has been made to include all known information on all Curwen locomotives of 7¼-inch gauge and above, inevitably further information will come to light after publication.

Any reader who has such details is invited to contact the author at the Old Bilsthorpe address; all relevant material will be passed to the Editor for consideration for publication.

THE MINIATURE LOCOMOTIVES OF DAVID CURWEN

CONTENTS

PUBLISHED MARCH 2008

INTRODUCTION

Anyone with even a passing interest in the miniature railway scene will probably be familiar with the name of David Curwen. With an active loco-building career spanning more than half a century, David can rightly be regarded as the *doyen* of the miniature locomotive world.

When it was announced in 2006 that David was writing his autobiography, enthusiasts looked forward to reading in more detail about his locomotives, but if they were expecting lists of Works Numbers, exact delivery dates and such, they were to be disappointed. The title of the book – "Rule of Thumb" (*) – accurately sums up David's approach to his chosen profession, i.e. to concentrate on working with tools rather than a pen! As a member of the old school of practical engineers, he had little or no time for record-keeping; fortunately (and somewhat to David's amazement), numerous enthusiasts have studied and recorded details of his work, making the tracing of all his locomotives somewhat less of a challenge than at first anticipated!

We believe therefore that this monograph, which has been published with the active support of David and his publisher David Edgington, includes every one of David's larger locomotives, albeit detailed information on one or two examples has yet to be unearthed. Hopefully our readers will fill in some of the gaps! (Lawson Little)

(*) See Appendix E for review of this book and ordering details.

A NOTE ON WORKS NUMBERS

As already mentioned, David had no time for detailed records, hence it is not surprising that there is no neat and tidy list identifying the fifty or more locomotives for which he was responsible. Hence we have chosen to record them under a series of reference numbers (1 to 54) arranged as far as possible in date order.

Of the locos which do carry works numbers, the following can be identified:-

1947 – 1949: locos given a number corresponding to their date of completion (or delivery – see discussion in Appendix B) i.e. 1548 = 1st May 1948.

1951 - 1964: no works numbers allocated, apart from two Atlantics numbered 2005 and 2006. This was clearly in connection with a short-lived scheme whereby earlier locos in the Baydon fleet were renumbered into a new series – see individual histories.

1965: one Atlantic reverted to original 'delivery/completion date' system.

1968 – 1975: locos numbered apparently at random (and many non-steam locos not numbered at all).

1976 – 1997: reverted to original "completion/delivery date" system.

THE MINIATURE LOCOMOTIVES OF DAVID CURWEN

The early years

David Curwen was born on November 30 1913, and became indoctrinated with steam at a very early age. His maternal grandfather was one of the first generation of naval engineers, serving at a time when steam was beginning to supplant sail on the high seas. His tales of steam must have impressed young Curwen, whose love of the subject was further fostered by lineside observations of the railway near his home at Sydenham.

At the end of World War One, David's family moved to Kent, where the young boy was able to continue train-watching on the South Eastern & Chatham Railway line a couple of fields away from his new home. His first 'hands-on' experience of railways was, like so many of us, with a Hornby train, but he soon aspired to something more prototypical; his father was 'something in the City' so was well able to afford a couple of guineas for a Bassett-Lowke O-gauge Caledonian 0-4-0 tender engine, steam powered of course. Powered by a meths burner, the loco performed admirably on a length of track laid on the carpet (!), and David was encouraged to save his pocket money in order to buy a more ambitious model. This was an L.M.S. 'Crab'

The first Pacific, 1547, at Hilsea. (Simon Townsend collection)

2-6-0, costing five guineas; for some long-forgotten reason it was powered by clockwork - at least it would have posed less of a fire hazard!

As time passed, other interests replaced trains – first motorcycles, then cars. The problems of keeping these relatively primitive machines road-worthy led to a life-long fascination with the internal combustion engine, so it was perhaps not surprising that after completing his schooling David became apprenticed to a local garage proprietor. Apart from maintaining road vehicles, he also learned the intricacies of small electricity generating plants, which in the inter-war years were quite commonly employed at isolated country houses.

After some years, David was ready for a new challenge; in 1935 he applied for a job with Short Brothers, the aircraft manufacturers at Rochester, Kent. Shorts' speciality was flying boats, and David spent the next ten years working on these, as well as the Stirling bomber and other wartime projects.

Working for himself - David Curwen Ltd.

After the war ended, he was released from his reserved occupation and, again ready for a change, formed a small engineering concern in partnership with Richard Ripley, a friend from aircraft company days. A neighbour, Stephen Brown, who farmed at Peasmore, near Newbury, also joined the firm; he shared David's interest in steam cars as well as railways.

Pacific 2647, running as No.2001, at Weymouth (June 1967). (N.Fields)

An earlier view of 2647/2001 at Weymouth (September 1959) - note the lipped chimney. (N.Fields)

Under the title of David Curwen Ltd., the new firm began business in 1946 in a rented corn store at Russley Park, Wilts, before moving to a former chicken house (owned by Stephen Brown) at Baydon, near Marlborough. Here David was able to revive his interest in locomotives – one of his first such tasks was to complete a part-finished 7¼-inch gauge GCR 'Immingham' 4-6-0 which had been started by a Mr Edgar Newbury. This loco (reference 46 in the Summary) was eventually sold to a Mr. Liversedge at Herne Bay after running for one season at the Steamer Pier, Weymouth.

Another early job was a 3½-inch gauge 0-6-0T built as a prototype for Bassett-Lowke, who planned to market it as a kit of parts for home assembly. Delivered to the London showrooms in unpainted brass finish, the model was declared 'too good to paint' and was kept on display there for many years.

Yet another project was a model of the Southern Railway S15 4-6-0, (1 in the Summary), built rather unusually to 7½-inch gauge rather than the more normal 7¼-inch; this appeared in 1947 and was supplied to the Folkestone Miniature Railway.

By that year the firm was employing half-a-dozen people, and its first substantial order came from Hilsea Lido, near Portsmouth, where a 10¼-inch gauge line was being operated using a hired locomotive. David recalls this as being of Bullock manufacture (it was in fact Pacific No.1003 "Western Queen", built by Bullock in 1934).

The line's proprietor was experiencing problems with the locomotive and asked David for advice. The latter thought the loco 'not up to the job'; in a 1986 letter to John Hall-Craggs he described it as "a bit light and skimpy". David's philosophy, which was to be followed throughout his working life, was that strong, simple construction was the most important aspect of locomotive design.

The customer specified another Pacific as a replacement, and after some deliberation David chose the then recently-introduced Edward Thompson LNER Class A2 4-6-2 as a prototype. This decision was influenced by a design study of the type by "LBSC" in Model Engineer, which attracted David as a well-thought-out project, though the loco's rather ungainly appearance, with a very compact coupled wheelbase and outside cylinders set well back behind the front bogie, is not to everyone's taste, particularly when compared to the elegant designs of Sir Nigel Gresley, Thompson's predecessor on the LNER. It is possible, however, that David chose the set-back cylinder design to allow the front bogie additional sideways movement, in order to cope more easily with tight curves.

At any rate, David and his team commenced work on not one but two Pacifics modelled on the A2, priced at £1,500 each according to the catalogue, with an extra £100 for an (optional) copper boiler. The second Pacific was intended for testing before transfer to a separate Company, Baydon Miniature Railways, which David had formed to exploit the demand for miniature railways at (mainly) seaside resorts. (See Appendix B).

The first Atlantic, 2448, at Bognor Regis - the name "Canadian Chief" is painted on the tender, and North American-type number boards fitted ahead of the chimney. The loco is painted in Canadian Pacific-style dark red livery. (Ray Wilkinson)

Atlantic, 5748, running as No. 750 "Blanche of Lancaster", pilots sister 2448 (No. 751 "John cf Gaunt") at Stapleford Park (September 1967) - both locomotives originally ran at Bognor. Th only visible difference between the two is the 'cowcatchers' (correctly 'pilots'), one of which has horizontal slats and the other vertical ones. (D.Trevor Rowe)

As an interesting aside, both Pacifics originally had plain double chimneys (which incidentally are dummies – only the front half of the chimney is used), but at some stage the second loco was fitted with a lipped one; the full-size Thompson examples on the L.N.E.R. varied in exactly the same way.

The two locomotives (2 and 3 in the Summary), were completed in the first half of 1947, works No's 1547 and 2647 being their respective dates of completion (or delivery - see discussion later). No. 1547 went to Hilsea and 2647 to the Baydon MR line at Weymouth, but prior to delivery they were inspected and reviewed for Model Engineer by J. N. Maskelyne. David gained the impression that the great man did not wholly approve of his work, since he had departed from prototype by fitting Baker valve gear (which David preferred as being simpler to machine and easier to dismantle) rather than the LNER-standard Walschaerts. There were other minor variations, generally made in the interests of 'fitness for purpose', and David concluded that in the eyes of the reviewer the Pacific in effect 'didn't have the right number of rivets' and therefore wouldn't win any prizes! Nevertheless as far as the builder was concerned, the locomotives 'were a good design, looked good and did the job'. The proof of the pudding is that sixty years later both still survive, one in full working order and the other soon to be so.

The Curwen Atlantics

Presumably following the publicity this work engendered, D.C. Ltd. received an order for two locomotives from a Mr. Briggs of Worthing, but rather than replicate the Pacific design, David thought that a four-coupled wheelbase would be more suitable for the sharply-curved tracks found on many miniature railways. Accordingly he revised the design into a 4-4-2, and since this wheel arrangement was inappropriate for the 'Thompson image' he 'free-lanced' the appearance in a fairly modest way. A raised footplate was incorporated, pre-dating the adoption by British Railways of this feature, along with a U.S.-style chimney and cab, second dome and bogie tender. David referred to this design as 'Americanised', but its distinctive appearance eventually made it known simply as the 'Curwen Atlantic'.

The new design was very successful, being strongly built and a good steamer; its main drawback was a certain lack of adhesion due to the centre of gravity being further back in the frames than was ideal (see later discussions on various attempts to remedy this). Initially a batch of five locos (ref.'s 4 - 8 in the summary) was put in hand, all destined for completion in 1948 or soon after. No.2448 went to Mr. Briggs for the Bognor Regis Miniature Railway, 3548 to the BMR line at Southend, and 4648 was exported to South Africa; 5748 was the second Briggs loco and

Atlantic 1149 is seen at Skegness, where it worked for a couple of seasons after the Southend line closed. (I. Gotheridge collection)

The "Coghlan" 0-4-2 1750 - an early view prior to rebuilding in GWR style. (Dave Holroyde collection)

1149 joined 3548 at Southend. The Atlantic for South Africa was first exhibited in steam on a stationary test stand at the 1948 Model Engineer Exhibition at Westminster, where it made its mark (literally!) in the form of a sooty patch on the ceiling!

According to the catalogue, the Atlantics were priced at £1,250 (again plus £100 for the copper boiler if fitted - boilers, incidentally, were subcontracted to Tom Goodhand of Gillingham). Other details listed in the catalogue were :-

Scale 2¼-inch to the foot (approx.)
Length 13ft 6ins overall
Weight 30cwt - 2 tons (loaded)
Driving wheels 13½-inch dia.
Bogie wheels 7¼-inch dia.
Trailing wheels 8¼-inch dia.
Cylinders 4.1/8 x 4.7/8-inch
Valve gear – Baker's design...can be removed in a few minutes for overhaul.
Very powerful steam brakes to driving wheels.
Tender of robust construction, mounted on two bogies or three axles.
Coal consumption 1cwt per day (Welsh steam coal for preference).

The Company also offered to supply trucks, bogies, track, signals, stations etc. Loco delivery was six months from date of order.

A paragraph in "MODEL ENGINEER" dated February 10 1949 is sufficiently interesting to be worth quoting in full –

"Recently we paid a visit to the workshop of Messrs David Curwen at Baydon, near Marlborough, Wilts., and were pleasantly surprised at what we found there. To begin with, the locale is unusual in that it is entirely surrounded by typical Wiltshire downland country, an ideal setting for a truly rural mode of life, rather than for a busy, if small, engineering workshop!

The shop itself consists of a large army hut of very robust construction, warm and weatherproof, well-lighted and comfortable. It is equipped with a well-chosen selection of lathes, millers, drilling machines and other tools, and power is derived from an oil engine which drives an electric generator. The staff comprises, perhaps, a dozen men.

Work was proceeding upon a number of locomotives ranging from 3½ to 10¼ inch gauge; most of these engines were in for seasonal overhaul and repair. A 10¼ inch gauge version of "Hielan' Lassie" was awaiting attention after about eight months of strenuous work at Weymouth (author's note: this would be 2647 "Robin Hood".)

An American-looking 4-4-2 engine for 10¼-inch gauge, similar to one exhibited at last year's M.E. Exhibition – illustrated on this page (photo is of 2448) - was under construction, and we were much interested in some novel features on it, especially its main axleboxes."

Sadly this flurry of activity was destined to be short-lived; the Baydon MR requirements had now been fulfilled, and for a while outside orders were slow to materialise. One of the last jobs in which David was personally involved here was the completion in 1950 of a 10¼ inch gauge 0-4-2 tender engine, which had been purchased from a Mr. Herbert Coghlan in a part-built state. This loco (47) had been planned as a 9½-inch gauge Caledonian 0-4-2T and was said to incorporate some Bassett-Lowke parts.

Otherwise work was slow, and perhaps recognising this, David sold his interest in the two concerns in 1951 to a Mr. Eric Carr, activities then being transferred to a site at Whittonditch near Ramsbury, a mile or two south of the Baydon premises. The firms continued to trade under the Curwen and Baydon names, however.

Talyllyn Interlude

In 1949 Roland Fuller, one of David's contacts at Bassett-Lowke, had introduced him to L.T.C.Rolt, who was currently investigating the possibility of converting the still just operational but very run-down Talyllyn Railway from 2ft 3-inch to 15-inch gauge. Coincidentally, David had recently married, and his wife Barbara was Rolt's cousin by marriage. Tom Rolt took David to Towyn, and the latter subsequently produced some costings for the planned conversion, but happily wiser counsels prevailed and the Talyllyn survived in its original form to become the world's very first preserved railway.

Talyllyn Railway No.5, seen immediately after delivery, in Towyn Yard. Tom Rolt is on the footplate, and his 1924 boat-tail Alvis is immediately behind the loco (September 1952). (T.R.)

That wasn't the end of David's connection with Towyn, however. Moving ahead to 1951, by which time a Preservation Society had taken over the Talyllyn Railway, Tom Rolt invited David to become Chief Mechanical Engineer of the line. He accepted the offer, and he and Barbara found accommodation in Wales. His subsequent experiences at Towyn are documented in Rolt's classic book "Railway Adventure" and are well worth reading.

Whilst challenging and no doubt interesting, the position at Towyn was financially less than ideal for a relatively newly-married couple, and at the end of the 1951 season David was forced to resign and move back to Wiltshire. Here he and Barbara found a pair of dilapidated cottages in the village of All Cannings, near Devizes (Barbara's father lived in the same village). David still maintained a close relationship with Tom Rolt however, and at the latter's request built for the Talyllyn a small petrol tractor for use on permanent way trains.

"T.R. No. 5" (14) was delivered in October 1952, and comprised a light steel frame fitted with TR wagon wheels, powered by a petrol engine and epicyclic gearbox removed from Rolt's narrow-boat "Cressy". Incorporated at Rolt's request, presumably to save money, this power unit (which had originally been fitted to a Model T Ford!) proved totally unsuitable for rail use, even on the light track-maintenance duties for which the loco had been designed.

No.5 had a short and chequered career on the Talyllyn; over the winter of 1952/53 it was used to provide a passenger service for local inhabitants, hauling one coach and the Corris van, and

Above: after a short and rather ignominious career, TR No. 5 stands awaiting dismantling. (L. Bedder via T.R.)
Below: reduced to a flat wagon and renumbered 19, TR No. 5 carries a weedkiller tank, and is recognisable only by the distinctive axleboxes. (T.R.)

it also worked p.w trains, but the day after one such foray just before Easter 1953 the ancient petrol engine was found to be seized solid. No.5 never ran again under its own power and in April 1954 it was stripped down to the frame and transformed into Wagon 19, in which guise it survives to this day.

Hence the widest (2ft 3-inch gauge) and shortest locomotive built by David Curwen also proved to be the least successful!

Back at Whittonditch, locomotive construction continued. There is an unconfirmed suggestion that a sixth 10¼-inch gauge Atlantic was built for export to Argentina or Peru (reference 9); several other locos which did appear during the 1950-52 period included a 7¼-inch gauge "Royal Scot", which was built for Bassett-Lowke (10), and more interestingly, an **18-inch** gauge version of the standard Curwen Atlantic (11) named "Crompton" and destined for the Fairy Glen MR at New Brighton. A May 1951 newspaper report (which incidentally confirms that David had left the firm by that date) quotes "Crompton" as being delivered the previous month, and mentions that two further Atlantics were under construction at that time. These would have been No's 2005 and 2006 (12 and 13 respectively), which were delivered in 1952 and proved to be the last known locomotives built by the firm before it was wound up (see Appendix B).

A scene at Skegness c.1952/53 with what is believed to be Atlantic 2005 – note the single dome (earlier Atlantics had two), also the unique deep valance to the footplate – a temporary addition? (I.Gotheridge collection)

Above: seen at New Brighton soon after delivery, "Crompton" in original condition, September 1952. (S.Townsend collection)
Below: By 1953 "Crompton" had been fitted with an LMS Coronation-style streamlined casing. Seen here with ex-Jaywick coaches. (C.P.Friel collection)

A new beginning - Curwen & Newbery Ltd.

When David returned to Wiltshire from Wales, he took the opportunity of purchasing a small general engineering business in Devizes, in conjunction with his friend, the previously mentioned Edgar Newbery. As acquired, the firm (which was then renamed Curwen & Newbery Ltd.) was tackling a remarkable variety of work, including agricultural drainpipe laying and the making of moulds for Avon Rubber, but not surprisingly attention eventually turned to the production of locomotives.

Initially these were i/c-engined machines, the first recorded being a freelance 0-4-0DM named "Belle", (15) built for Sir Thomas Salt in 1954 and fitted with a Petter AVA1 diesel engine. This passed through several hands but is now safely preserved by an NGRS member.

Some years passed before the next locos appeared, but in the early '60's the firm produced a pair of 7¼-inch gauge "Warship" 4-4wPH locos powered by BSA 250cc engines. One was purchased by Strathaven Council for use on the Strathan MR (16) and the other went to the Strand MR at Gillingham (18). The latter appears to have gone in part-exchange for a Great Central Atlantic chassis together with a Bassett-Lowke 7¼-inch gauge LNWR "George The Fifth" 4-4-0; David rebuilt the latter before selling it through Christies in London for £750 (a sale he apparently later regretted).

David Curwen's first non-steam effort was this Petter-engined four-wheel diesel, seen after complete restoration by its current owner Gordon Brown, August 2006. N.R.Knight)

Warship "The White Heron" at Stapleford Park, August 1995. (DWH)

A few years later Strathaven came back for another "Warship" (24) and at about the same time David was approached by Lord Gretton, the Bass Brewery magnate. Lord Gretton had purchased two of the original Curwen Atlantics (2448 and 5748 both ex Bognor Regis) for his 10¼-inch line at Stapleford Park, near Melton Mowbray, and, clearly impressed with their workmanship, asked whether an i/c-engined loco could be supplied for the same line.

The result was a scaled-up version of the Strathaven "Warship", fitted with a Vauxhall 1200cc. petrol engine, which was named D100 "The White Heron". (17) Although re-engined a couple of times, it is still working on the same line.

Not rail-related, but worth mentioning as an indication of David's "can do" attitude, was a further enquiry from Lord Gretton as to whether Curwen & Newbery could build a miniature passenger-carrying ocean liner to provide a service on the lake at Stapleford Park! Nothing daunted, David sketched out a small-scale copy of the liner "Northern Star", only to discover that in places the lake was only 12 inches deep. At this point David must have remembered a contract he had carried out for his then wife-to-be's father many years ago, which involved fitting paddle wheels to ex-Army landing craft to make them suitable for use as canal houseboats. He applied the same technology to the liner design, the paddle wheel being concealed at the rear of the vessel,

Above: the second Curwen liner "Southern Cross" on the lake at Stapleford Park. This is actually the Severn-Lamb built example, which for some reason seems to feature in most known photos, but "Northern Star" is believed to have been identical.

Below: the first "Western" at the Payton Heights Railway, Margate, running as No. 1 "Lady Sonia" (July 1994). (DWH)

Another Western, D1011 "Western Thunderer", seen at Audley End where it ran for forty years. (July 1994). (Dave Holroyde))

which when completed could from a distance almost be taken for the real thing! The design was so successful that a repeat order was secured some years later, which David sub-contracted to Severn-Lamb Ltd. as "Southern Cross". Sadly both liners were laid up after the death of Lord Gretton; one eventually rusted away to scrap, and the other was removed for restoration which is believed never to have been completed.

By 1962 Edgar Newbery was in his '70's and decided to retire. His share of the business was eventually sold, in the process of which David effectively lost control of the Company, which became part of a larger group. Over the next few years the firm completed a trio of "Western"-class 6-6w locos with a variety of transmission systems. 1964 saw the appearance of a diesel-mechanical example fitted with Perkins 4.99 engine (19) for Margate MR. Another '64-built loco with a Ford 100E 1172cc petrol engine and mechanical transmission was built for the Audley End MR, Essex (20) and the following year a similar-powered machine but with hydraulic drive went to the Minehead MR (21). All these were 10¼-inch gauge.

Also in 1965, the firm produced two 10¼-inch steam locos; the first was a revival of the 1948 "Curwen Atlantic" design for Lowestoft MR (22), the second a scale model of a Great Northern Atlantic for Audley End (23).

Above: after a thirteen-year gap, a final Curwen Atlantic appeared in 1965. Built for the Lowestoft Miniature Railway, No.1865 is seen running there in September 1971. (DWH collection)

Below: David Curwen's first steam "scale replica", a fine representation of a Great Northern Ivatt Atlantic, also appeared in 1965, and is seen looking just as good twenty-five years later, in May 1990. (DWH)

On his own again

Despite all this activity, David was unhappy with a situation where he was effectively working for others, not a position he relished, so in 1966 he resigned to form a design consultancy in partnership with Dennis Plowright, a contact from Avon Rubber days. Together the two were soon occupied providing engineering solutions to production problems encountered by various big-name companies.

Fortunately this type of work allowed David to continue manufacturing locomotives at his home at All Cannings, once described in print as "the world's only thatched-roof loco works"! Much of his work was destined for the previously mentioned Audley End MR, whose owner The Hon. Robin Neville (now Lord Braybrooke), became (and remains) a close personal friend. Over a twenty-year period David produced a whole series of locomotives, both steam and i/c, for the Audley End line.

David also now found time to design locomotives on behalf of other builders, in particular Severn-Lamb Ltd., who produced more than three dozen engines of Curwen design.

The first major job for the "All Cannings Loco Works" was a 7¼-inch gauge Denver & Rio Grande Western Class K36 2-8-2 (25), which David built for the late Brian Hollingsworth, ordered after Brian had been impressed by the two Atlantics at Stapleford. The K36 appeared in 1967; the following year David built a freelance 0-6-0PM "diesel shunter" (26) for a customer in Sussex.

The first of the Denver & Rio Grande K36 2-8-2, 487, under construction in David's workshop in 1967. (D Burwell collection)

Above: another view of 487 during construction.

Below: Mikado No. 487 after delivery. (both D.Burwell collection

Above: yet another Western, D1017 "Western Warrior", seen along with scale rolling-stock on the Garden & Woodland Railway, Oxon, where it has worked successfully for thirty years. (DWH collection)
Below: the second K36 was sold to the Forest Railroad at Dobwalls after the original customer cancelled. Named "General Palmer", it is seen waiting for customers in the main station at a point where four separate circuits run in parallel. Sadly, this line closed in 2006. (Lawson Little)

Above: another Dobwalls loco was No. 8 "David Curwen", seen here after the addition of a leading truck. The D&RGW "Road-Switcher" is seen behind. (July 1976). (DWH collection)

Below: the freelance 0-4-0T+T "Brock", seen here on the Downs Light Railway, May 2001. (DWH)

0-4-2 "Dickie", named after Dickie Murdoch who performed the naming ceremony, at Beer Heights. (J.MacDougall)

Also in 1968 David received his first order from John Southern, who was creating an extensive 7¼-inch line at Dobwalls, in Cornwall. For this line David produced another "Western" 'diesel' loco, actually powered by a Fiat petrol engine (27). This loco had a fairly brief stay at Dobwalls before being sold, not due to any failings but because John Southern had decided to "Americanise" the line and therefore disposed of his British-style stock.

John came back to All Cannings for a more suitable loco for the new image, which duly appeared in the shape of a Bo-Bo "Road Switcher", also of Denver & Rio Grande lineage. This loco (28) was powered by a BMC A-series petrol engine, but the Dobwalls line was also looking for U.S.-style steam power, so when a customer for whom David was building a second K36 2-8-2 decided to cancel his order, David was able to sell it on to John Southern. For one season, this loco (29) ran in harness with its twin on loan from Brian Hollingsworth's line.

The next project was a freelance 0-6-0 tender engine (ref.30), in "plantation" style, yet again for Dobwalls; for a while this carried the name "David Curwen". It was subsequently rebuilt as a 2-6-2, then a 2-6-0.

Another freelance loco followed in 1975, this time an 0-4-0T+T, supplied to J.I.C. Boyd for the Downs Light Railway at Colwall, Hereford. Unusually for David, this loco (31) was built to 9½ inch gauge.

The following year three more locos emerged from David's workshop. The first was an 0-4-2

Above: the K36 design was scaled up to 10¼-inch gauge for the Audley End Railway. Numbered 489 and lettered for the Rio Grande, the loco is seen at Audley End. (Alan Bowler)

Below: this freelance Mogul named "Isambard Kingdom Brunel" was built for Penwith Park, Cornwall. (N.R.Knight)

Above: David's first 12¼-inch-gauge loco was built for service in France but has spent most of its working life on the Fairbourne Railway in Wales. (D.Trevor Rowe)
Below: also built for France but never delivered there, 0-6-4ST "Beddgelert" was styled after a Welsh Highland prototype. Seen here at Barmouth Ferry on the Fairbourne Railway, August 1995. (S.Townsend)

tender version of the ex-Corris Railway "Douglas" (32), supplied to the Peco line at Beer, Devon, and this was followed by a pair of Kerr-Stuart-type 0-4-2ST's (33, 34), one for a Midlands-based doctor and the other for David's own use. All were 7¼-inch gauge.

Having built a couple of 7¼-inch gauge Rio Grande 2-8-2's, David felt confident enough in the soundness of the design to suggest to Lord Braybrooke that a 10¼-inch gauge example would be suitable for Audley End, and just such a loco (35) appeared in 1977. David's other project that year was a freelance Mogul (36), again 10¼-inch, for the Age of Steam Park in Cornwall. Interestingly, thirty years later a second loco to this design is under construction at the Royal Victoria Railway (54) using David's design and patterns.

In 1978 (the year incidentally when David reached the official 'retirement age'!) things 'moved up a gear' with the production of two 12¼-inch gauge engines for John Ellerton, who was building a line, the Reseau Guerledan Chemin de Fer Touristique, in Brittany. The first, a half-sized replica of the well-known Manning Wardle Lynton & Barnstaple 2-6-2T, was actually delivered to France but the second, modelled on a Welsh Highland 0-6-4ST and completed in 1979, never crossed the Channel due to the premature closure of the French line. After several years in store it was eventually reunited with its companion when the Reseau Guerledan stock was transferred to Fairbourne and John Ellerton narrowed the former 15-inch gauge Welsh line to suit his locos. (37 and 38).

David's only K37 Mikado followed its smaller sister to Dobwalls, where it became No. 498 "Otto Mears". (LL)

As a matter of interest, John Milner records in "Rails Through The Sand" that David also produced no fewer than thirty pairs of 12¼-inch gauge bogies for all the passenger coaches on the French line. David also built complete coaches to accompany some of his locos, notably at Stapleford.

In 1980 John Southern came shopping again for another U.S.-style steam loco for Dobwalls. The K36's had proved their worth there, but to provide something slightly different David produced a replica of the even larger K37 2-8-2 (39); the full-size K37's had actually started life as standard-gauge locos but were rebuilt to 36"-gauge when the Rio Grande needed heavier power in the late 1920's, and although narrow gauge, were (and still are, in preservation) equivalent in size and power to a British 8F 2-8-0!

In 1981 David was occupied in rebuilding one of his earliest locos, Atlantic No. 3548, which had passed through a number of hands (and been "modified and altered by all and sundry" as David comments in his book!). The loco had been purchased by Lord Braybrooke as long ago as 1964, but after working successfully for many years was found to dislike some of the heavy gradients on a recent extension of the Audley End line. David therefore undertook to rebuild it as a 2-6-2; in the process a new boiler was fitted, the latter incidentally carrying a chimney and dome identical to those fitted to the 7¼-inch Rio Grande locos. The rebuilt loco was named "Lord Braybrooke".

The following year yet another Mikado appeared on the scene, when David delivered a 7¼-inch K36 (40) to Bob Smith, a Scottish customer. Though David would not have realised it at the time, this turned out to be the last loco he produced for anyone apart from Lord Braybrooke, since he was to spend the rest of his working life building engines for the Audley End line.

483, another K36, went to Scotland, where it is seen on the Comrie Railroad. (DWH collection)

The "Scale Model" period

The next Audley End project was a relative "quickie", a simple 0-6-0PM shunter (41) powered by an Austin engine. This was followed by something of a tour de force in the shape of a scale model of a Great Western "Star"-class 4-6-0, accurate even to the extent of being fitted with four cylinders. As David has stated, to achieve such accuracy demands a great deal more effort than producing a workaday design and the time-scale necessary is "at least twice as long". Whilst the resultant loco can be described as museum-quality, it is not necessarily suitable for the rough-and-tumble of everyday commercial work, and the Audley End team has recognised this by placing the Star on display rather than using it regularly.

Because of the complexities of the design, not to mention the fact that David was now in his seventies, this loco (42) was not delivered until 1989, but his next effort for Audley End, a 10¼-inch version of a Sandy River & Rangeley Lakes 2-6-2 (43) was completed relatively quickly, being delivered in 1991.

Yet another "scale model" was the next to appear, in the shape of a London & Northwestern "George the Fifth" 4-4-0 "Loyalty". This very fast machine (44) is the personal steed of Lord Braybrooke.

"Doris" is a small petrol-engined shunter built for Audley End, though it takes its turn on lighter passenger trains too. (September 2002) (D.Trevor Rowe)

Above: perhaps David's finest achievement was this scale-replica Great Western "Star" 4-6-0, built like the prototype with four cylinders. Seen prior to being placed on permanent indoor display, May 1990. (DWH)

Below: a handsome American design is this replica of a Sandy River 2-6-2, built for Audley End, April 1992. (N.R.Knight)

Above: another scale replica is this L&NWR "George V"-class 4-4-0 "Loyalty", built for Lord Braybrooke and used at Audley End, April 1995. (N.R.Knight)

Below: David's last large loco was named after his wife, the design being based on the Ffestiniog Railway "twins" Linda" and "Blanche" but with the addition of a trailing truck. Seen here on home rails at Audley End in May 1998. (DWH)

When "Loyalty" was delivered in 1994, David was eighty years old, but still had the energy to tackle one final project for his friend. Delivered early in 1997, his swan song was a 2-4-2ST+T based on the Hunslet twins "Linda" and "Blanche" as rebuilt by the Ffestiniog Railway. It is an indication of the regard felt at Audley End for the builder that this loco (45) is named "Barbara Curwen".

Thus finally ended a working career, which, as far as large locomotive building is concerned, had spanned some fifty years, surely a record for one man! This brief account has concentrated almost entirely on locos of $7\frac{1}{4}$-inch gauge and above, but David has also been responsible for a number of smaller ones. Indeed even in his eighties he helped Lord Braybrooke build a 5-inch gauge "garden railway", producing a simple Kerr-Stuart "diesel shunter" for the line, as well as many scale lineside buildings (some incorporating scale-sized bricks!).

As well as actually building locos, David has also been responsible for designing for other manufacturers, specifically: -

Reference 48 "Muffin" 0-6-0 designed for Longleat, built by Berwyn Engineering
49 "Western"-class 6-6w for Severn-Lamb Ltd.
50 "Shelagh of Eskdale" 4-6-4DH for Severn-Lamb Ltd.
51 0-6-2T ("Zebedee"-class) for Severn-Lamb Ltd.
52 Rio Grande steam-outline 2-8-0 for Severn-Lamb Ltd.
53 "Modified Western"-class 4w-4 for Severn-Lamb Ltd.
54 Replica of Freelance 2-6-0 ref.36, under construction 2007 by Royal Victoria Railway using DC patterns.

See Appendix D for details of all the above.

The fifth (and largest) "Western"-class loco produced by David was "Princess Anne" built to 15-inch gauge for the Lakeside MR at Southport, where it is seen in August 2001. (DWH)

SUMMARY OF LOCOMOTIVE PRODUCTION
(7¼-inch gauge and larger)

Ref.	Date(s)	Gauge-inches	Wks.No	Type	Power	Notes
1	1947	7½	-	Southern S15 4-6-0	Steam	
2	1947	10¼	1547	Curwen Pacific 4-6-2	Steam	
3	1947	10¼	2647	Curwen Pacific 4-6-2	Steam	
4	1948	10¼	2448	Curwen Atlantic 4-4-2	Steam	
5	1948	10¼	3548	Curwen Atlantic 4-4-2	Steam	
6	1948	10¼	4648	Curwen Atlantic 4-4-2	Steam	
7	1948	10¼	5748	Curwen Atlantic 4-4-2	Steam	
8	1949	10¼	1149	Curwen Atlantic 4-4-2	Steam	
9	?	10¼	?	Curwen Atlantic 4-4-2	Steam	1
10	1951	7¼	-	"Royal Scot" 4-6-0	Steam	
11	1951	18	?	Curwen Atlantic 4-4-2	Steam	3
12	1952	10¼	2005	Curwen Atlantic 4-4-2	Steam	2
13	1952	10¼	2006	Curwen Atlantic 4-4-2	Steam	2

"Muffin" was designed for the line at Longleat, but has spent most of its life on the Lappa Valley Railway in Cornwall, where it was pictured in May 2005. (Peter Groom)

"Shelagh of Eskdale" is a one-off in several respects; very unusually for a diesel loco, it is of 4-6-4 configuration rather than having powered bogies, and it also has proper "sit-in" cabs. Built for Ravenglass, where it is seen in August 2005. (DWH)

14	1952	27	-	Freelance 4wPM	Petrol	
15	1954	10¼	-	Freelance 0-4-0DM	Diesel	
16	1962	7¼	-	"Warship" 4-4wPH	Petrol	
17	1962	10¼	-	"Warship" 4-4wPM	Petrol	
18	1963	7¼	-	"Warship" 4-4wPH	Petrol	
19	1964	10¼	-	"Western" 6-6wDM	Diesel	
20	1964	10¼	-	"Western" 6-6wPM	Petrol	
21	1965	10¼	-	"Western" 6-6wPH	Petrol	
22	1965	10¼	1865	Curwen Atlantic 4-4-2	Steam	
23	1965	10¼	-	GNR Atlantic 4-4-2	Steam	4
24	1966	7¼	-	"Warship" 4-4wPH	Petrol	
25	1967	7¼	-	DRGW K36 2-8-2	Steam	5
26	1968	7¼	4	Freelance 0-6-0PM	Petrol	
27	1969	7¼	370	"Western" 6w-6wPM	Petrol	
28	1970	7¼	41	DRGW Road-Switcher	Petrol	
29	1971	7¼	39	DRGW K36 2-8-2	Steam	
30	1972	7¼	47	Freelance 0-6-0	Steam	
31	1975	9½	751	Freelance 0-4-0T+T	Steam	
32	1976	7¼	976	Freelance 0-4-2	Steam	
33	c.1976	7¼	-	Kerr-Stuart 0-4-2ST	Steam	
34	c.1976	7¼	-	Kerr-Stuart 0-4-2ST	Steam	
35	1977	10¼	772	DRGW K36 2-8-2	Steam	
36	1977	10¼	577	Freelance 2-6-0	Steam	

37	1978	12¼	1078	Lynton & Barns. 2-6-2T	Steam	
38	1979	12¼	1279	Welsh Highland 0-6-4ST	Steam	
39	1980	7¼	1780	DRGW K37 2-8-2	Steam	
40	1982	7¼	7582	DRGW K36 2-8-2	Steam	
41	1982	10¼	682	Freelance 0-6-0PM	Petrol	
42	1989	10¼	-	GWR "Star" 4-6-0	Steam	
43	1991	10¼	491	Sandy River 2-6-2	Steam	
44	1994	10¼	-	LNWR "George V" 4-4-0	Steam	
45	1997	10¼	197	Hunslet 2-4-2ST+T	Steam	
46	1947	7¼	-	"Immingham" 4-6-0	Steam	9
47	1950	10¼	1750	Freelance 0-4-2	Steam	8
48	1967	15	-	"Muffin" 0-6-0	Steam	7
49	1967-71	10¼	-	"Western" 6-6w	Var.	6
50	1969	15	-	"Shelagh of Eskdale"	Diesel	6
51	1970-74	15	-	0-6-2T	Steam	6
52	1971-87	Var.	-	Rio Grande 2-8-0 s/o	Var.	6
53	1972-81	Var.	-	Modified "Western" 4w-4	Petrol	6
54	2007	10¼	-	Freelance 2-6-0	Steam	10

Cleethorpes No.800 is one of the less-common "Mark II" versions of the popular Severn-Lamb Rio Grande 2-8-0. It was also unusual in being propane-powered and built to 14¼-inch gauge. (G.Clarke collection)

Notes:

1) Rumoured sale to South America - not confirmed
2) Building date uncertain - c.1952
3) Carried numbers 39112/9111-3/1953
4) Works Plates marked "Doncaster 1172/1907" as per prototype
5) Works Plates marked "Baldwin 58588/1925" as per prototype
6) Designed for and built by Severn-Lamb Ltd. (2-8-0's are steam-outline with petrol, gas or diesel engine).
7) Designed for Longleat and built by Berwyn Engineering Ltd.
8) Part-built by Herbert Coghlan, completed by D.C. Ltd.
9) Part-built by Edgar Newbery, completed by D.C. Ltd.
10) Under construction 2007 by Royal Victoria Railway using DC patterns.

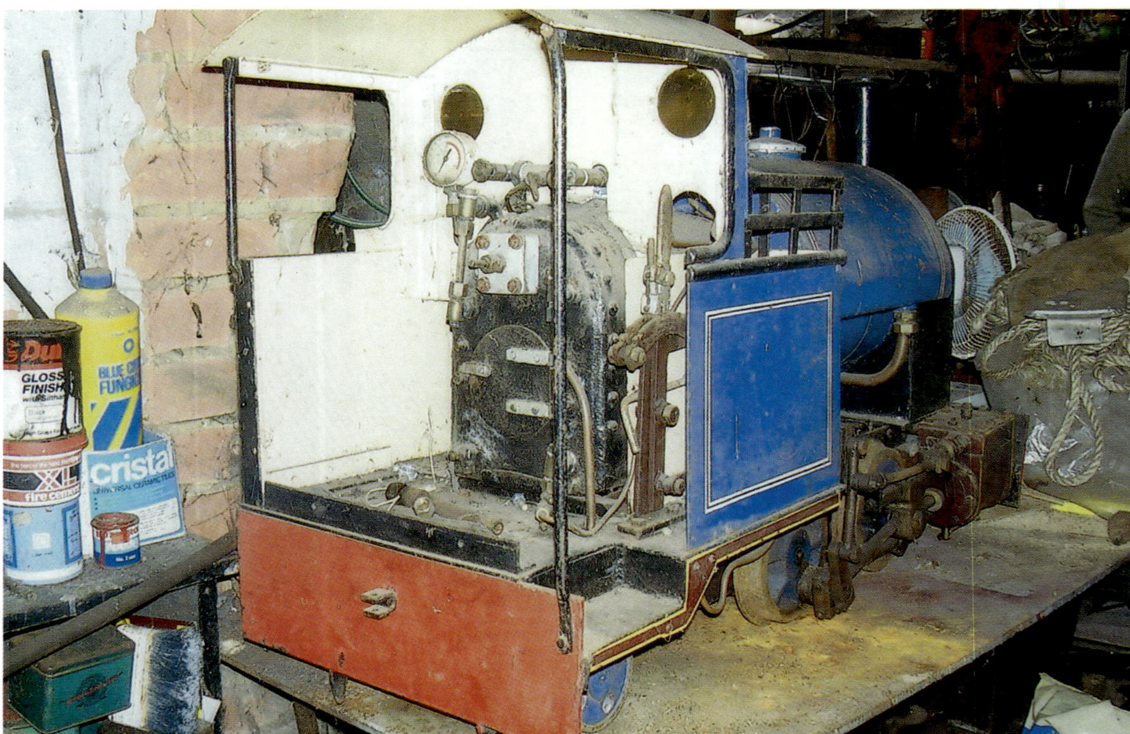

A very recent view inside David's workshop, featuring the "Kerr-Stuart" 0-4-2ST which he built for his own use, designed after 'Talyllyn No. 4'. (Helen Allenby)

INDIVIDUAL LOCOMOTIVE HISTORIES

N.B. Throughout the following section, these abbreviations apply:

DC.Ltd. - David Curwen Ltd.
C&N - Curwen & Newbery Ltd.
DC - David Curwen

MR – Miniature Railway
BMR – Baydon Miniature Railways

(Note regarding the locos owned/operated by BMR: it was the firm's practice to return these to Baydon when required (probably every close season) for overhaul/repainting as required. These movements have not been included in the individual histories)

1) Southern Railway Class S15 4-6-0

Built to 7½-inch-gauge by DC.Ltd 1947. No Works No. Fitted Baker valve gear. Originally numbered 3, named "Lord Radnor".

Supplied new to Folkestone MR.
1954 to Colonel Tyrrell, New Romney, Kent.
c.1962 to Sir. J. Samuel, Greywood Central Railway, Walton-on-Thames and rebuilt there by Dick

David's first large loco was this handsome Southern Railway S15 4-6-0, seen in later life after being rebuilt with Walschaerts valve gear. (C.Bishop)

Simmonds and Fred Stone to 7¼"-gauge. Original Baker valve gear replaced by Walschaerts pattern.
1966 to C.J.Bishop, Great Cockcrow Railway, Chertsey, as No. 837.
Still there 2007.

Current status: Serviceable (used summer months only). Still carries original Goodhand boiler, has had a few copper firebox stays replaced but passes annual inspection without difficulty.

Current livery: Lined green, lettered "Southern" on tender, no name.

2) 1547 Curwen Pacific 4-6-2

Built to 10¼-inch-gauge by DC.Ltd. 1947, Works No. 1547
Based on LNER Thompson Class A2 Pacific, Fitted Baker valve gear, Goodhand boiler.

Supplied new to Hilsea Lido, Portsmouth as 1547. Newspaper photo confirms the loco as being nameless when delivered, but a later view shows nameplates in situ on the smokebox – unfortunately the name is not readable, but the word lengths confirm that it was not "William Bell" at that time (possibly "Lady Peggy"?).
Later returned to DC Ltd. and by 1949 at Lakeside MR, Carr Mill, St.Helens, where renumbered 1946 and named "William Bell" (presumably after Mr. Bell, proprietor of the Lakeside line).
c.1953 to Drayton Manor Park, Fazeley, Staffs, as No. 11, name retained.
By 1967 to J.H.Rundle Ltd. (dlr), New Bolingbroke, Lincs, altered to 4-6-0 to cope with sharp curves on private line. Number reverted to 1946. Only steamed once each year, and not at all after 1980's.
7/05 on loan to Kirkby Green Light Railway, Sleaford, for restoration.

Current status: new boiler fitted and steam test passed 8/07. Complete top end overhaul and repainted in crimson lake. Still numbered 1946 and named "William Bell". In service on Kirkby Green Light Railway from 27/8/07.

The first Pacific 1547 when brand new at Hilsea (J.Hall-Craggs collection)

Above: not a very clear view but the only one available showing "William Bell" at the Lakeside MR, St. Helens (not to be confused with the Southport line of the same name). (N.Knight collection)

Below: "William Bell" in a rather sorry state at Rundle's yard, August 1973. (N.Knight)

Above: happily restored to its former glory, "William Bell" has its very first public steaming for forty years at the Kirkby Green Light Railway in Lincs. (August 27 2007). The proud driver is custodian Stuart Ravell. (N.Knight)

Below: another sad sight, "Robin Hood" after rescue from Weymouth by Jack Doyle. Seen in his workshop, January 1972. (N.Knight)

3) 2647 "Robin Hood" Curwen Pacific 4-6-2

Built to 10¼-inch gauge 1947 by DC.Ltd. 1947, Works No. 2647. Identical to ref. 2 above.

Supplied new to Weymouth MR. By 1959 renumbered 2001.
By 1971 the line was owned by a branch of the Chipperfields Circus, and the loco had been out of use for some time. In September of that year it was purchased by Jack Doyle, Burnage, Manchester, in a "package deal" with Atlantic 2005 – Jack only wanted one loco but had to take both or neither! He retained 2005 as being a more practical proposition for use on his proposed portable line, and sold the Pacific to R.Holliday, Waterbeach, Cambs, a driver at the Audley End Railway; it was delivered to Coleby-Simkins at Stapleford Park for overhaul prior to going to Essex.
/72 - /74 steamed occasionally at Audley End.
-/74 to M. Bamford, Ashbourne, Derbys.
-/80 to Oakhill Manor Railway, Somerset.
12/04 to J. Nemeth Engineering, Severn Beach, Glos.

Current status: undergoing complete overhaul for two private owners for a new line in Berkshire. Currently numbered 2647 and retaining original name. Livery L.N.E.R. Doncaster Green.

Only a couple of years later, "Robin Hood" is again resplendent in LNER green after overhaul by Coleby-Simkins. Seen in steam at Audley End, where its owner was a driver, August 1973. (N.Knight)

The first Curwen Atlantic No.2448, seen at Stapleford after being named "John of Gaunt", March 1978. (N.Knight)

4) 2448 "Canadian Chief" Curwen Atlantic 4-4-2

Built to 10¼-inch gauge by DC.Ltd 1948, Works No. 2448. Shortened and "Americanised"(*) version of ref.3.

Supplied new to S.R.Briggs, Bognor Regis MR in red livery.
-/50 line closed, loco stored.
c. /55 to P.Harding-Kiff (dlr), Mablethorpe.
12/57 or 3/58 to Lord Gretton, Stapleford MR, Melton Mowbray where renumbered 751 and renamed "John of Gaunt ".
Winter 1969 - Major overhaul and numerous modifications by Coleby-Simkins. Original Goodhand boiler replaced by new one supplied by Gowers of Bedford (reputed to be their last job before closure).
1987-91 - Further major overhaul and modifications by R.Coleby.
16/9/95 renamed "John H.Gretton".

(*) "Americanisation" (DC's term) comprised raised running plates, two domes (usually), U.S-style chimney and cab, bogie tender, "cowcatcher" etc.

Richard Coleby has very kindly supplied detailed notes on the modifications carried out to this locomotive in 1969 and 1987, and these are reprinted in full in Appendix A.

Current Status: in use (#). Still named "John H. Gretton" and numbered 751, apple green livery, lettered S.M.R.

(# N.B. The Stapleford Miniature Railway is a private line and only opens to the public on (usually) two weekends each year. Dates are published in advance in NARROW GAUGE NEWS).

Above: the only visible difference is the enclosed valve gear, but 2448 was a very different loco by August 1998 (see Appendix A). (B.Hillsdon).

Below: Atlantic number two was renumbered 2271; seen here at Coate Water, Swindon after initially working at Southend. (S.Townsend collection)

5) 3548 Curwen Atlantic 4-4-2

Built to 10¼"-gauge by DC.Ltd 1948, Works No. 3548. Exactly as ref. 4 above.

Supplied new to Baydon Miniature Railways line at Southend.
By 7/52 transferred to BMR line at Coate Water, Swindon, where running as No. 2271.
By 3/64 to Audley End Railway, Saffron Walden at a cost of £750, where named "Bobbie", later renamed "Gordon". Tender lettered "Audley End Railroad", LNER green livery.
Loco ran successfully for many years at Audley End, but when the line here was extended in 1979, the amended route included a steep gradient which found the Atlantic struggling for adhesion, hence the rebuild below.
-/81 completely rebuilt by D.C. as 2-6-2, frames lengthened at rear, new cab, boiler mountings replaced by taller versions (identical to 7¼"-gauge K36). Renamed "Lord Braybrooke", retained no. 3548, but repainted GER blue.

Current status: in use. Currently painted mid-green with black and yellow lining.

Above: Lettered "Audley End Railroad" in acknowledgement of its trans-Atlantic appearance, 3548 is seen prior to its rebuilding as a 2-6-2. (N.Knight)

Right: the Works Plate on 2-6-2 3548. (AER)

Above: completely transformed after rebuilding by David, 3548 now carries the name of its owner, Lord Braybrooke, April 1994. (N Knight)

Below: "The One That Got Away" – David's only direct export, Atlantic 4648 "Sarie Marais" at the Florida Lake MR, Johannesburg, October 1959. (B.Nicholson collection)

6) 4648 Curwen Atlantic 4-4-2 "Sarie Marais"

Built to 10¼"-gauge by DC. Ltd. 1948. Works No. 4648. Exactly as ref. 4 above.
Boiler Inspection Certificate dated 28th May 1948 to allow loco to be exhibited in steam at the Model Engineer Exhibition.
Supplied new to Bernard James, Florida Lake MR, Florida, Johannesburg, South Africa, where numbered 1948 (and later possibly 2010).
1970 to C.F.Marais, still at Florida Lake.
-/03 to Deon Taljaard, Johannesburg, where numbered 2010.

Current status: being overhauled. Deon states that the boiler is "still perfect today".

4648 undergoing a major overhaul by owner Deon Taljaard, May 2007). (D.Taljaard)

7) 5748 Curwen Atlantic 4-4-2

Built to 10¼"-gauge by DC.Ltd 1948, Works No. 5748.

Supplied new to S.R.Briggs, Bognor Regis MR.
-/50 stored by Briggs after line closed.
c. /56 to P.Harding-Kiff, Mablethorpe, (dlr).
12/57 or 3/58 to Stapleford MR, Melton Mowbray, where later running as
No. 750 "Blanche of Lancaster".
-/75 to Pritchard, Worksop, Notts.
10/84 to Suffolk Miniature Light Rwy, Kessingland. Reboilered c.1986 (boiler by David Vere, Sheffield).
11/87 to Bickington Steam Rwy, Liverton, Devon.

Current status: Not steamed since 1997. Currently under overhaul, loco presently unpainted (previously blue), tender still lettered S.M.R.

Above: Stapleford's other Atlantic, "Blanche of Lancaster", seen here on a nostalgic return visit there after twenty years absence August 1995. (S.Townsend)

Below: the fifth Atlantic was 1149, seen here when named "Minx" at Exmouth, June 1964. (J.H.Meredith)

Thirty years on but still with Exmouth tender lettering, the loco has been renamed "Emily" and is seen running on the North End Railway in Wilts. (July 1998). (B.Hillsdon)

8) 1149 Curwen Atlantic 4-4-2

Built to 10¼"-gauge 1948 by DC.Ltd. Works No. 1149.

Supplied new 1949 to Southend MR (BMR)
c. /52 to Skegness MR (BMR)
c. /53 returned to Baydon.
-/60 to Exmouth MR, Devon, where running as No. 2003 "Minx".
-/67 to J.Morley, Claverdon, Warwicks.
-/73 to North End Rwy., Ashton Keynes, Wilts, where named "Emily".
-/00 to Private Owner, Wilts.

Current status: stored serviceable. Green livery, lined red. Tender still lettered Exmouth Miniature Railway. Retains No. 2003 and name "Emily".

9) -?- Curwen Atlantic

Rumoured to have been sold to Argentina, or possibly Peru (from a comment by the late Stephen Brown to John Hall-Craggs). Confirmation required.

10) LMS "Royal Scot"-type 4-6-0

Built DC Ltd. 1951 to 7¼" gauge.

Supplied new to Bassett-Lowke Ltd., Northampton for E.Pardoe, Biarritz, France.
c. /70 to Waller, Meopham, Kent.
c. /73 to Frampton, Berkswell, Coventry.
c. /86 to Frampton, c/o Hollycombe Steam Collection, Liphook, Hants where named "Robert Kennaway".

Current status and location: unknown

Above: this Royal Scot 4-6-0 was built on behalf of Bassett-Lowke, and is seen here at Liphook when named "Robert Kennaway" c.1995. (B.Lee)

Below: "Crompton" soon after delivery to New Brighton, c.1952. The ex-Jaywick coaches are behind the tender. (B.Gent collection)

A later view of "Crompton" after the fitting of an LMS-style streamlined casıng, October 1959. (D.Chatfield)

11) No. (-)* Curwen Atlantic 4-4-2 "Crompton"

Built to 18" gauge DC Ltd. 1951. Enlarged version of "Curwen Atlantic" and much modified to cope with 40ft-radius curves – "not designed to go fast or far"! Stated to weigh 3¼ tons when new, "Crompton" was an ungainly brute, its appearance not helped by the apparent use of a standard boiler, necessarily raised high above the chassis to match the larger loading gauge. David has never recognised the loco as "one of his"!

Supplied new 4/51 to Fairy Glen MR, New Brighton as "Crompton".
Carried various numbers - 3-9112, 9111-3 and 1953.
C.1953 fitted with streamlined boiler casing in style of LMS "Coronation" class; this was removed after 1959.
2/66 to W. Morris, Bromyard.
10/77 to S. Symonds, Worcs.
6/85 to J.Selway, Bloxwich.
C.12/92 same owner, Wednesbury.
4/05 on loan (minus tender) for display at Cleethorpes Coast Light Railway.

Current status: stored awaiting full restoration.

12) 2005 Curwen Atlantic 4-4-2

Built DC Ltd. c.1952. Works No. 2005. Only one dome on boiler.

Supplied new to Skegness MR. (BMR)
c. /53 returned to Baydon then transferred to Weymouth MR by 8/53 where named "Black Prince" and

Above: Atlantic 2005 at Skegness. (S.Townsend collection)

Below: after a couple of years at Skegness, 2005 went to Weymouth, where it is seen here September 1959. (J.H.Meredith)

numbered 2005. Worked extremely hard there – up to 14 hours per day, seven days a week in season! Out of use by 1971.
9/71 to Jack Doyle, Burnage, Manchester along with Pacific 2647 (which see). Steamed occasionally on portable track at Dinting, Poynton and other locations in Manchester area, but found to be too heavy for regular portable use, so resold to Tony Allcock by 7/73.
Tony and a colleague completely rebuilt the loco, in the process "Anglicising" its appearance by lowering the footplate and fitting new cab and smoke deflectors along with a British-style chimney. Tony also added an ashpan, the loco having previously run without the benefit of this feature, as well as proper side-control for the front bogie; the original copper boiler was retained however. A detailed account of the various modifications appeared in the issues of MODEL ENGINEER dated 5th and 19th April 1974.
The rebuilt loco, now named "Waverley", numbered 196, and painted in North British-style brown livery, was used on the "North Midland Railway", which ran between the standard-gauge station and loco sheds at Loughborough (Great Central). By 1975 alterations to the (main line) track layout at Loughborough necessitated closure of the 10¼" line, and "Waverley" was sold to Graham Ellis, Isle of Mull, and stored for use on the under-construction Mull & West Highland NGR.
Reboilered (boiler by David Vere, Sheffield) 1987 whilst in store.
1993 in service on Mull & WHNGR, Craignure, Mull. Like other locos of this design she suffered from lack of adhesion in inclement conditions, and in an attempt to alleviate this, old lead pipes from Torosay Castle were cast into ingots and bolted between the frames. Despite this she saw only limited use on Mull, where larger locos of narrow-gauge outline (which allowed the driver to shelter inside the cab in poor weather) were preferred.
1994 rebuilt by David Vere, Sheffield.
1997 sold to Waverley Group but remained on Mull
5/03 to Waverley Group, c/o Rudyard Lake Rwy, Staffs.
11/03 to Bo'ness & Kinneil Rwy, Scotland, for overhaul.
27/8/05 returned to Rudyard Lake.

Current status: In use. Numbered '1' and retains name "Waverley", tender still lettered M.R., painted Caledonian Blue.

Specification: Driving Wheels 13" dia. Boiler Pressure 160psi. Loco weight in working order 1½ tons.

Totally unrecognisable after being "anglicized" by Tony Allcock, 2005 is seen at Loughborough in August 1973, in North British livery and named "Waverley". (N.Knight)

"Waverley" now resides on the Rudyard Lake Railway after a spell in Scotland. (October 2003) (J. Hawkesworth)

13) 2006 Curwen Atlantic 4-4-2 "Merrie England"

Built to 10¼"-gauge by DC Ltd c.1952, Works No. 2006.

As previous Atlantics but at some stage (almost certainly from new) fitted with 'streamlined' shrouds over cylinders and under running plate at cab end (see special note below). Only one dome on boiler.

c. /53 to Weymouth MR (BMR) painted cream (probably the most impractical livery on a steam locomotive since the London & North Western Railway painted a Webb Compound white for Royal Train duties!). Named "Merrie England" after Councillor England, the line's liaison officer at Weymouth Council.
c. /64 to Private Owner, Sutton Coldfield.
By 8/75 same owner, Aberystwyth. Still there 8/95.

Current status: unknown. Assumed in store, the line here has been disused for at least twenty years.

Special note:- the question of streamlined shrouds on Curwen Atlantics is a matter of some debate amongst enthusiasts. Included in this book are photos showing what is believed to be 2005 at Skegness, fitted with a straight valance along the full length of the running plate, and 2006 at Weymouth with very curved valances at front and rear. The writer has also seen another photo (unsuitable for reproduction) showing a cream-painted Atlantic in the yard at Whittonditch with curved valances of a quite different pattern. The latter view, unfortunately not dated, also shows several other Atlantics (along with 0-4-2 1750) all apparently freshly painted, so most likely was taken at the end of a close season after the Baydon fleet had received their winter overhauls. This does not explain why the style of valance was apparently altered. See also John Knightbridge's comments in Appendix A.

Above: a poor shot but the only one available of the curiously-embellished and garishly-painted "Merrie England" at Weymouth. No wonder the operator preferred the Pacific! (DWH collection ex James Slater)

Below: Talyllyn No. 5 being prepared for its first trip on the line. (TR)

14) Talyllyn No. 5 : 4-wheel Petrol Tractor

Built DC 1952. Comprised new steel frame on Talyllyn wagon wheels, powered by petrol engine and epicyclic gearbox originally fitted to a Model T Ford car and previously used in Tom Rolt's narrow-boat "Cressy".
Delivered new 10/52 to Talyllyn Railway.
Unsuccessful due to effectively only having one gear in each direction, it was intended for use only for light p.w. work, but after being pressed into service on passenger trains the engine seized and the loco never ran again under its own power. Dismantled 4/54 and chassis used for Wagon No. 19.

Current status: after years in general use as a flat wagon or part of the weedkiller train, No. 19 is now semi-retired, and can usually be found parked on the wharf at Tywyn carrying a generator. The only remaining evidence of its former life as a locomotive is a large toothed cogwheel bolted to the rear of one wheel.

Above: TR No. 5 on its designed duties, a permanent-way train, October 1952. (TR)
Below right: now semi-retired, Wagon 19 (ex Loco 5) carries a generator on the Tywyn Wharf siding. (TR)
Below left: seen after withdrawal, this view illustrates the 'TALYLLYN RAILWAY 5' lettering. (TR)

"Belle", fully restored and resplendent on the Somerford Light Railway (August 2006). (N.Knight)

15) 0-4-0DM "Belle"

Built 1954 to 10¼"-gauge, fitted from new with Petter AVA1 diesel engine (contrary to many published reports).

Supplied new to Sir Thomas Salt, Shillingstone, who numbered her '1' and reputedly named her after his favourite sow!
c.7/75 to Crowlas Woodland Railway, Crowlas, Cornwall, where later renamed "Kingsley".
c.12/82 to P.A.Hanton, Congleton.
c.7/85 to P.A.Hanton, Rudyard Lake Railway, Staffs.
10/6/2000 to G.Brown, Somerford, Congleton.

Current status: in use, green livery with black and yellow lining and red frames. Original name "Belle" restored, and numbered '1'.

Additional note: the late Peter Hanton recounted to Gordon Brown that when he collected the loco from its previous owner, it was stored in a 'quarry'. As it was being loaded, a workman asked Peter if he had the plates, and assuming this was a reference to the "Kingsley" ones, Peter replied in the affirmative. Only later did he realise that the man probably meant the original "Belle" plates, which, together with the metal letters "S.L.R." which Sir Thomas had personally cut and fitted, could have been stored nearby. (Gordon Brown has made and fitted replacement nameplates and lettering).

"Belle" was used in the construction of the Rudyard Lake Railway, and subsequently "worked to death" on passenger trains, but when Peter Hanton retired through ill-health and the line was sold, he honoured a long-standing promise that Gordon Brown could buy the loco. As a "basket case", it had to be completely stripped down before being rebuilt to its present immaculate condition.

Gordon subsequently had an interesting 'artefact' passed to him by Sir Thomas' son – a galvanised steel plate, professionally lettered "Powered by Petter Diesel" (the Petter name is rendered as the Company logo). The plate has four mounting holes and was clearly intended to be fitted on the loco, but for some reason this was never done, and fifty years later the plate was finally passed to Gordon, still in its original packaging.

16) BR "Warship"-class 4-4wPH

Built by C&N 1962 to 7¼"-gauge. BSA petrol engine, hydraulic transmission.

Supplied new to Strathaven Council 3/6/62, for use on Strathen MR, Scotland where named "Wee Jock".
c. /83 to R.Fuller, Uddingston, Glasgow, where rebuilt with Honda engine.
1/94 to Alderney MR, Mannez, Alderney, C.I., where named "HMS Alderney" and numbered D872.
Rebuilt by A. Tucker to 4w-4wPH 1996.
11/98 to J.Tucker, Surrey.

Present status: under restoration.

17) BR "Warship"-class 4w-4wPM

Built by C&N 1962 to 10¼"-gauge, fitted Vauxhall Viva 1200cc engine.

Supplied new with six coaches to Stapleford MR, Melton Mowbray where named "The White Heron" and numbered D100. Delivered in primer and painted dark blue by Hon. John Gretton (despite the name, it has remained blue ever since!).
-/72 rebuilt Coleby-Simkins with Ford 100E 1172cc engine
By /95 again rebuilt, with Ford 1600cc engine.

Current status : still in use at Stapleford.

An early view of "The White Heron" (always painted blue despite its name) at Stapleford Park. (N.Knight)

Another "Warship", this time 7¼ -inch gauge, after purchase by Chris Fincken (November 1990). (DWH)

18) BR "Warship"-class 4-4wPH

Built by C&N 1963 to 7¼"-gauge. BSA 250cc petrol engine, hydraulic transmission.

Supplied new to Strand MR, Gillingham, Kent.
Later rebuilt by Dick Cushing, Rainham, Kent with Petter diesel engine.
c.80/81 to C. Fincken, St. Albans.
12/87 to C. Fincken, Bromyard, Worcs.
6/94 to National Railway Museum, York (on loan) numbered D871 by 11/95.
c.5/97 returned to Bromyard.

Current status : in use, B.R. maroon livery, still numbered D871.

On loan for exhibition at the National Railway Museum, the Warship was also used on the short passenger-carrying line there (March 1997). (DWH)

The first "Western" diesel was built for Margate. Seen here after arrival on the Royal Victoria Railway, Netley, now named "Western Independence" and painted in Desert Sand livery (September 2007). (P.Bowers)

19) BR "Western"-class 6-6wDM

Built by C&N 1964 to 10¼"-gauge, fitted Perkins 4.99 diesel engine.

Supplied new to Margate MR.
By 5/75 to A.Pay, Payton Heights Railway, Margate, where named "Lady Sonia" and numbered '1'.
Out of use by 1988.
3/03 to Royal Victoria Railway, Netley, Hants, where rebuilt with Kubota engine and hydraulic transmission. Repainted in "Desert Sand" livery, numbered D1000 and renamed "Western Independence".

Current status: in use as 6-6wDH.

The first "Western" diesel soon after arrival on the Royal Victoria Railway, Netley, March 2005. (B.Gent)

Above: the second Western, "Thunderer", put in forty years hard work at Audley End but has recently moved to join her sister at Netley. (D.T.Rowe)
Below: A recent view of "Western Thunderer" (May 2005). (P.Henshaw)

20) BR "Western"-class 6-6wPM

Built by C&N 1964 to 10¼"-gauge. Fitted Ford 100E 1172cc engine.

Supplied new to Audley End Railway, Saffron Walden as D1011 "Western Thunderer".
12/04 to P.Bowers, Royal Victoria Rwy, Netley,

Current status: in use. Maroon livery with yellow square on ends.

21) BR "Western"-class 6-6wPH

Built by C&N 1965 to 10¼"-gauge. Fitted Ford 100E 1172cc engine.

Supplied new to Minehead MR, Somerset as "Exmoor Enterprise".
By 6/65 returned to C&N for repair following derailment!
Out of service c.1989.
10/91 to Knebworth Park MR, Herts. Not used here but stored on site until moved to L.A.Services Ltd. for overhaul.

Current status: still under repair.

22) 1865 Curwen Atlantic 4-4-2

Built C&N 1965 to 10¼-gauge, reviving the original "Americanised" design
Supplied new to Lowestoft MR as 1865.
1974 to A.B.Mason, Burnham Market.
1981 to R.Dale, Louth, Lincs.

Current status: stored (has not been steamed for many years). Red livery.

The newest Curwen Atlantic was built in 1965 for Lowestoft, where it is seen in an early view. (DWH collection)

Above: for more than twenty years 1865 has been in Lincolnshire, painted red and lettered LNER – surely a contradiction! (June 1987). N. Fields)

Below: David Curwen's first "scale replica", a fine Ivatt Atlantic, built for Audley End and seen there in May 1990. (DWH)

The GNR Atlantic in use at Audley End, with Lord Braybrooke at the regulator, April 1992. (N.Knight)

23) 4433 Great Northern Atlantic 4-4-2

Built C&N 1965 to 10¼"-gauge. Scale replica of GNR Atlantic (LNER Class C1), fitted prototype-pattern works plates lettered "Doncaster 1172/1907", numbered 4433.

Supplied new to Audley End MR, Saffron Walden, Essex.

Current status: in use. Green livery.

24) BR "Warship"-class 4-4wPH

Built by C&N 1966 to 7¼"-gauge . BSA engine.

Repeat order from Strathaven Council, delivered Spring 1966.
Withdrawn 1975 and later broken up for spares.

25) Denver & Rio Grande Class K36 2-8-2

Built DC 1967 to 7¼"-gauge. Scale replica of 3ft-gauge prototype preserved in Colorado, fitted prototype-pattern Baldwin Works Plates numbered 58588/1925.

Supplied new to B.Hollingsworth, Beaconsfield, Bucks, as No. 487 Queen of Colorado".
8/72 on loan to Hilton Valley Rwy, Hilton, Shrops.

c.4/73 on loan to Forest Railroad, Dobwalls, Cornwall.
-/73 returned to B.Hollingsworth, Croesor Jct. & Pacific RR, Penrhyndeudraeth, Gwynedd.
11/94 to C.Fincken, Herefords.

Current status: under repair, was due to re-enter service 2007. Black livery, retains original name and number, works plates lettered "Curwen Locomotive Works, Devizes, England No. 487, 1967"

Above: K36 No. 487 soon after delivery. (DWH collection)

Below: bad place for a derailment! No.487 suffers a minor mishap whilst in use on Brian Hollingsworth's line in Wales, October 1993. (N.Knight)

A more recent view of 487 at its present home in Herefordshire. (DWH)

26) Freelance 0-6-0PM

Built by DC 1968 to 7¼"-gauge. Works No. 4.

Supplied new to G. C. Hudson, West Chiltington, Sussex.
c. /86 to Cheals Garden Rwy, Pulborough, Sussex as No. 1280.
c.8/90 returned to G. C. Hudson.
c. /96 to A. S. Reen, Yapton, Sussex.
1996 to Hollycombe Steam Collection, Liphook, Hants, owned by P. & L. Collins.

Current status: believed operable.

27) BR "Western"-class 6-6wPM

Built by DC 1969 to 7¼"-gauge. Works No. 370. Fitted Fiat 500 engine.

Supplied new to Forest RR, Dobwalls, Cornwall as D1017 "Western Warrior"
1973 to Brean Central Rwy, Brean, Somerset.
c. /76 to Earle, Bristol.
c. /78 to E. Martin, Garden & Woodland Rwy, Oxon.

Current status: in use, retains original name, maroon livery. Owner has fitted a small lawnmower carburettor and modified the induction hotspot, which has more than halved fuel consumption. Otherwise "...in most respects this loco is too well thought out for us to muck it about...!"

Above: "Western Warrior" in front of the imposing engine shed on the Garden & Woodland Railway in Oxon. (DWH collection)

Below: described as a "Rio Grande Road-Switcher", Dobwalls No. 108 betrays its origins as a British Rail Class 20, modified to transatlantic appearance during construction to suit the change to American emphasis at Dobwalls (July 1976). (DWH)

28 Denver & Rio Grande Western Road Switcher 4-4wPM

Built by DC 1970 to 7¼"-gauge. Works No. 41, fitted BMC A-Series engine.
Apparently planned originally as a British Railways Class 20, body design revised to suit customer's American preference.
Supplied new to Forest RR, Dobwalls, Cornwall. Numbered 108.
1981 on loan to Beach Lawns MR, Weston-Super-Mare, numbered 3039.
1981 returned.
5/87 on loan to Malvern Hills Animal & Bird Garden, Malvern.
9/87 returned.
1988 on loan to Buckfastleigh MR, Devon.
1988 returned.
c. /89 to Malvern Hills again.
Line later closed, and loco stored.
2006 - sold to Private Owner, Worcs.

Current status: unknown

Yet another K36 was No. 488 "General Palmer", seen here at Dobwalls in July 1976. (DWH)

29) D&RG K36-class 2-8-2

Built by DC 1971 to 7¼"-gauge. Works No. 39.

Supplied new to Forest RR, Dobwalls, Cornwall, as No. 488 "General Palmer". (General Palmer was the founder of the Denver & Rio Grande Railroad).

Current status: still at Dobwalls, condition unknown.
Intended for use on a planned new line here in the future, hence not included in 11/07 auction.

Above: the "plantation-style" "David Curwen" started life as an 0-6-0, in which form it is pictured at Dobwalls in July 1976. (DWH)
Below: after a spell as a 2-6-2, "David Curwen" reappeared as a 2-6-0, as seen here in June 2004 shortly before leaving Dobwalls. (DWH)

30) Freelance 0-6-0

Built by DC 1972 to 7¼" gauge. Works No. 47.

Supplied new to Forest RR, Dobwalls, Cornwall.as No. 8 "David Curwen" (originally to be named "Daffodil"!).
Later rebuilt to 2-6-2, then to 2-6-0 (by -/86). By 9/87 renumbered 88.
C.8/05 to -?-, Witney, Oxon.
12/06 advertised for sale by Station Road Steam, Lincs.
1/07 to Eastleigh Lakeside Railway.

Current status: in service.

This freelance 0-4-0T+T was built for the Downs School, Colwall where it is pictured in May 1992. (DWH)

31) Freelance 0-4-0T+T

Built by DC 1975 to 9½" gauge. Works No.751

Supplied new to J.I.C.Boyd, Downs School, Colwall, Herefords.. as "Brock".

Current status: in use. Blue, black and red livery, retains original name.

32) Freelance 0-4-2

Built by DC 1976 to 7¼" gauge. Works No. 976.

Supplied new to Beer Heights LR, Beer, Devon, as No. 3 "Dickie". In service 1977.

John MacDougall, Chief Mechanical Engineer at the Beer Heights Light Railway, has kindly supplied the following details:

"Dickie" is based loosely on "Douglas" of the Talyllyn Railway; the original intention was to name the locomotive "Douglas Junior" (nameplates were cast and still exist). However when the late Richard "Dickie" Murdoch offered to perform the naming ceremony in 1977, the name was altered, and is still carried.

"Dickie" at the Beer Heights Light Railway, Beer c.1993. (J.MacDougall)

The loco was reboilered in 1992/93, and in addition has had three major overhauls, necessary because it has covered more than 20,000 miles at Beer! Work has included replacement of driving wheels and pony truck, crank webs and pins, motion brackets, part of rear mainframe, and tender drag box and footplate, as well as the new boiler. Originally painted bright red, "Dickie" subsequently appeared in black livery, was later apple green, and currently is Caledonian Blue with white lining.

Loco specification includes: 10"dia. driving wheels; 10.75"dia saturated boiler pressed to 100 p.s.i.; Walschaerts valve gear; 104 sq.in. grate area; cyls. 3½" x 4½".

33) Kerr Stuart-type 0-4-2ST

Built by DC c.1976 to 7¼" gauge for own use. Based on KS 4047/21 (now Talyllyn No. 4).

By 7/77 on loan to Age of Steam, Penwith Pleasure Park, Crowlas, Cornwall, returned 2/87.

Current status: in store at All Cannings. The garden trackage here was lifted many years ago; it included a short tunnel of such tight dimensions that on one occasion Tom Rolt was knocked out whilst driving this loco through it!

34) Kerr Stuart-type 0-4-2ST

Built by DC c.1976 as twin to above, supplied to a doctor in the Midlands. No further information available.

Above: a recent view of David's own locomotive. A 7¼-inch gauge version of Talyllyn No.4, It is believed to have dropped a plug (in other hands) when last steamed many years ago, and David has always been too busy to get round to repairing it. (Helen Allenby)

Below: "Sara Lucy", a 10¼-inch gauge version of the popular K36 design, is the mainstay of the Audley End Railway, where it is seen in May 1990. (DWH)

35) D&RG K36-class 2-8-2

Built by DC 1977 to 10¼" gauge. Works No. 772.

Supplied new in 1978 to Audley End Railway, Saffron Walden, Essex, where numbered 489 and named "Sara Lucy" after one of Lord Braybrooke's daughters. Has been the mainstay of the line ever since, being much larger and more powerful than any of the other locomotives here. Built to ⅓rd-scale and weighs 2½ tons in working order.

Current status: in use, black livery, lettered Rio Grande on tender.

Above: the works plate from "Sara Lucy". (AEP)

Below: this neat little freelance Mogul was built for the Age of Steam line at Penwith Pleasure Park, Crowlas, Cornwall. (J.Doyle)

36) Freelance 2-6-0

Built by DC 1977 to 10¼" gauge. Works No. 577.

Supplied new to Age of Steam, Penwith Pleasure Park, Crowlas, Cornwall, as No. 4, "Isambard Kingdom Brunel".
c. /84 stored at Camborne, Cornwall.

Despite still being lettered 'P.P.P.' for previous owner Penwith Pleasure Park, this view was taken at its current home, the Royal Victoria Railway in August 2007. (P.Henshaw)

By -/92 stored at Old Music Museum, Goldsithney, Cornwall.
4/97 to J.Price, c/o Exmoor Steam Rwy, Bratton Fleming, Devon.
Dismantled for repair but this was not proceeded with.
/97 to Royal Victoria Rwy, Netley, Hants. Acquired as a 'set of parts' and completely rebuilt with many new items; fortunately the boiler only needed re-tubing.
-/07 after ten years continuous service, withdrawn for a further total rebuild, which included new wheels and the replacement of all running gear. The tender was completely rebuilt, with virtually only the original frames remaining.

Current status: still under repair, scheduled for completion by end 2007. Painted Mid-Brunswick Green, lettered R.V.R., retains original name and number.

SPECIAL NOTE: this loco is so well regarded at Netley that David Curwen was approached regarding the possibility of the Royal Victoria Railway building a second, identical, locomotive. See Appendix E for further details.

37) Lynton and Barnstaple type 2-6-2T

Built by DC 1978 to 12¼" gauge. Works No. 1078.

Supplied new to Reseau Guerledan, Mur de Bretagne, France, as No. 1078 "Jubilee".
c.12/84 to Fairbourne Rwy, Gwynedd. Later renumbered '1'; renamed "Yeo". Again renumbered E759 in 1985.
Plates on loco marked 'NWNGR Fairbourne 1/86'. (Original Works Plates with no. 1078 still in place).

Current status: in use. Painted in Southern Railway green with black and yellow lettering as per Lynton & Barnstaple appearance in S.R. days.

n.b. loco design is based on Manning Wardle 1361/97.

Above: Lynton & Barnstaple-type 2-6-2T "Yeo" on the Fairbourne Railway, with the beautiful Mawddach Estuary as a backdrop, May 2007. (DWH)

Left: the works plate from "Beddgelert" (October 2007). (LL).

Below: "Beddgelert", styled on a Welsh Highland design, stands on the traverser at Fairbourne, October 2007. (LL)

38) Welsh Highland type 0-6-4ST.

Built by DC 1978/79 to 12¼" gauge. Works No. 1279.
Follows appearance of the WHR locomotive "Beddgelert".

Supplied new to order of Reseau Guerledan, Mur de Bretagne, France, but not shipped there due to premature closure of the line caused by local difficulties. Instead stored at Milner Engineering, Rossett, Clwyd. Carried No. 1279 and name "David Curwen".
Finally delivered to Fairbourne Rwy, Gwynedd 2/84. Renumbered '2' and renamed "Beddgelert". Number removed by 8/90.
Plates on loco marked 'NWNGR Fairbourne 2/87' (Original Works Plates with no. 1279 still in place).

Current status: serviceable but relegated to spare loco for 2007 season – very well worn and due for complete overhaul 2008. Painted in black livery with red lining.

39) D&RG K37-type 2-8-2

Built by DC to 7¼" gauge 1980. Works No. 1780.

Supplied new to Forest RR, Dobwalls, Cornwall as No. 498 "Otto Mears".

Current status: unknown, however it is reported that the loco was due to be auctioned at Dobwalls 11/07, following the closure of the railway there.

The "Scottish K36" 483 at its home base of Comrie, Perthshire, September 1996. (DWH)

(Note:- the prototype Class K37 was introduced on the D&RG in the late 1920's when larger power was needed, and comprised ten Baldwin standard-gauge 2-8-0's dating from 1902 which were rebuilt as three-foot gauge Mikados. The prototype K37 is noticeably larger than the K36 but not significantly more powerful.)

40) D&RG Class K36-type 2-8-2

Built by DC 1982 to 7¼" gauge. Works No. 7582.

Supplied new to Bob Smith, Comrie Railroad, Perthshire.
Original DC worksplates removed from smokebox 2007, to be refitted elsewhere on loco. Replaced on smokebox by replica Baldwin plates carrying appropriate works no. for the '483' carried on the cabside (BLW 58584/25).

We are advised that the loco was a joint effort between DC and the customer, with the latter responsible for the tender, cab and air pump. No. 483 usually operates around fifteen times each year and has proved very successful and trouble-free.

Current status: in use. Black livery as prototype with graphite smokebox, also red driving wheels, 'Rio Grande' "speed lettering" on tender.

Freelance 0-6-0DM "Doris" is the maid-of-all-work at Audley End. (Lord Braybrooke)

41) Freelance 0-6-0PM

Built by DC in 1982 to 10¼ " gauge. Works No. 682.

Supplied new to Audley End Rwy, Saffron Walden, Essex.

Fitted Austin 1100 engine and gearbox, mounted crosswise as in the car. Drive taken to a layshaft between the frames onto the centre driving axle and thence via coupling rods to the other axles. Named "Doris" and used as general shunter at Audley End but also takes turns on passenger trains up to eight coaches.

Current status: in use. Green livery with "wasp stripes" on ends.

Pride of the Audley End line is "Polar Star", seen here prior to being placed on semi-permanent indoor display (April 1992) (N.Knight)

42) Great Western "Star"-class 4-6-0

Built by DC to 10¼" gauge, delivered 1989. No works plates.

Supplied new to Audley End Rwy, Saffron Walden, Essex as No. 4005 "Polar Star". Loco is a "scale model" fitted with four cylinders as prototype, and built to the special order of Lord Braybrooke. Being built to scale proportions it is not considered suitable by its builder for everyday commercial use, and in fact has been on display in the Estate Office since around 1990.

Current status: still on display.

Above: originally named "Linda", this replica of a U.S. Sandy River & Rangeley Lakes Railroad 2-6-2 is lettered for its prototype. (July 1994). (DWH)

Below: differences in scale are illustrated by this shot of Sandy River No. 24 alongside "Western Thunderer" at Audley End, July 1994. (DWH)

43) Sandy River 2-6-2

Built by DC to 10¼" gauge. Works No. 491.

Supplied new in 1991 to Audley End Rwy, Saffron Walden, Essex. Design based on the Sandy River & Rangeley Lakes Baldwin 51803/19. Delivered as No. 24 "Linda", name removed by 5/98.
By 9/02 renamed "Bruce" after Lord Braybrooke's Black Labrador.

Current status; in use. Black livery with white trim, still numbered 24, tender lettered "S. R. & R. L.".

44) London & Northwestern "Loyalty" 4-4-0

Built by DC to 10¼" gauge. No Works No., plates marked "LNWR Crewe April 1913".

Supplied new in 1994 to Audley End Rwy, Saffron Walden, Essex as a scale replica of an LNWR "George V"-class 4-4-0. This is Lord Braybrooke's personal steed, and is reputed to be 'very fast'.

Current status: stored unserviceable, last used 2006 but boiler certificate expired. Black L&NWR livery with red/yellow/grey lining.

Another scale replica, David's last, is this splendid London & North Western "George V" class "Loyalty", used by Lord Braybrooke as his 'personal steed' until withdrawn in 2006 with an expired boiler certificate, September 1996. (N.Knight)

Above: paired with the GNR Atlantic, "Loyalty" in use at Audley End (July 1996). (N.Knight)

Below: David Curwen's last large loco is appropriately named after his late wife Barbara. Seen here at Audley End in May 1998. (DWH)

45) Ffestiniog-type Hunslet 2-4-2ST+T

Built by DC 1996/97 to 10¼" gauge. Works No.197.

Based loosely on the Ffestiniog Railways Hunslet 2-4-0ST+T's "Linda" and "Blanche", (HE 590/93) but with added rear pony truck.

Supplied new to Audley End Rwy, Saffron Walden, Essex, as "Barbara Curwen".

Current status: in use. Painted maroon.

(It is worth noting that David Curwen was 84 years old when he built this loco!).

See Appendix E for details of the locomotives designed by David and built by others.

LOCOMOTIVES STARTED BY OTHERS BUT COMPLETED BY DC LTD.

46) Great Central Railway "Immingham"-type 4-6-0

Started by Mr. Edgar Newbery, completed by DC Ltd 1947 to 7¼" gauge.
Ran for one season at the Steamer Pier, Weymouth.
Then sold (according to "Rule of Thumb") to a Mr. Liversedge of Herne Bay.
No further trace.

0-4-2 No. 1750 began life as a set of parts for a 9½-inch gauge 0-4-2T but was transformed before completion into a more useful 10¼-inch gauge tender loco for use on Baydon Miniature Railway lines, originally at Swindon and later at Exmouth. Seen here at Exmouth in August 1966. (J.H.Meredith)

47) Freelance 0-4-2 No. 1750

Commenced by Herbert Coghlan (*), Newbury as a 9½"-gauge Caledonian 0-4-2T with Goodhand boiler and possibly incorporating Bassett-Lowke GNR Atlantic parts, but sold incomplete to DC Ltd. in exchange for a set of 15"-gauge wheels and cylinders(#). Completed 1950 to 10¼" gauge with a six-wheeled tender added. No Works Plates but 1-7-50 stamped on boiler.

Supplied new to Coate Water MR, Swindon (a Baydon Miniature Railways line), where it may have run as No. 2272.
Returned to Baydon after one season,
1953 to Exmouth MR, numbered successively 1750, 2, 9, 4782. Tender lettered 'LMS' by 1966.
c.-/68 to G. M. Densham, North Tawton MR (private line), Devon (in exchange for a i/c loco). Rebuilt with GWR-style cab and chimney, lowered drivers seat and longer frames.
1969 to private owner, North End Railway, Ashton Keynes, Wilts.

Current status: laid up serviceable after thirty years successful service at this location. Named "Marjon" after owners children, Brunswick Green livery.

Later, 1750 was rebuilt in Great Western style, as seen in July 1998. (B.Hillsdon)

(*) Herbert Henry Coghlan A.M.I.M.E, F.S.A. (1896-1981) worked in various rail-related positions in Burma and India after an initial period at Inchicore, Dublin. In later years he lived at Boxford near Newbury, and became Honorary Curator of Newbury Museum. His main claim to fame was the production of more than fifty books and papers on his hobby of Ancient Mining & Metallurgy, with the Royal Anthropological Institute..

(#) It is not known whether the 15"-gauge parts were ever built into a complete locomotive, but the mention of 15" is intriguing, since none of the Curwen-associated Companies ever built a steam loco to this gauge. The parts were possibly from an uncompleted cancelled order.

(Thanks to Brian Hillsdon for the above biographical note)

APPENDIX A: MODIFICATIONS TO CURWEN ATLANTIC 2448

(Kindly supplied by Richard Coleby, who has been associated with the Curwen locomotives at Stapleford Park for many years)

Of the many modifications which have been carried out over the years to the Curwen Atlantic, most of them were made during two major overhauls. The first took place over the winter of 1969 in the workshops of Coleby-Simkins Engineering, which were located on the estate at Stapleford Hall, and the second during 1987-89 after the Stapleford Miniature Railway had closed to the public and all the rolling stock put into store.

The first overhaul was carried out under the personal direction of the late John Gretton; the second resulted from a design briefing given to Richard Coleby by John Gretton who subsequently commissioned him to carry out the work. Very sadly, John did not live to see the locomotive in steam but hopefully would have been happy with the outcome of his basic ideas.

1969

The two Curwen Atlantics running at Stapleford, "*Blanche of Lancaster*" and "*John of Gaunt*", were always very sound engines, popular with the drivers and often to be seen double-heading the heavy boat trains up the Bank during the late afternoon period. However, the design of these engines with the cylinders set well back in the frames (as per Thompson) and the wide firebox, means that the centre of gravity is only just in front of the rear driving axle. This can result in a yawing ride and insufficient weight on the front bogie to be able to utilise it for a sensible side-control force to minimise the yawing and improve the curving at speed.

Also, the exhaust pipework from the cylinders ran a somewhat tortuous path through commercial right-angle bends, which gave the impression at least that there might be a higher back-pressure than was strictly desirable. This latter of course, would mean that the engine was not delivering all the power that it should be capable of, a matter that was anathema to John!

With Coleby-Simkins now established on the premises, so to speak, John at last had the opportunity to put his design ideas into practice so at the end of the '69 season No. 751 was brought into the works for a complete strip-down.

The work carried out was as follows: -

1) A specially-cast weight was added between the driving wheel tunnel axleboxes. This had extended lips to rest on the top of the boxes, just cleared the underside of the boiler cladding, and went as deep as practically possible and the maximum width that could be accommodated between the frames. This was purely to add adhesion weight, and played no part in the re-balancing.
2) A steel box was made up that sits just forward of the front drivers and extends between the cylinders, of a width that just allows for the modified exhaust pipes to pass between the box and the inside face of the frames.
3) Two further steel blocks, 2x 3x 12 inches long, were bolted to the inside of the frames forward of the cylinders.

4) The exhaust pipes were modified by putting short-turn elbows on each cylinder and running formed pipes, of a larger internal diameter, forward to a combining 'Y' under the smokebox before turning upwards with a specially made elbow into the blastpipe.
5) The motion work was left unchanged apart from fitting Nylatron bushes to the siderods, and re-bushing where required.
6) To take advantage of the extra front-end weight, a re-designed side control was added to the front bogie with much longer springs to provide plenty of adjustment without overstressing.
7) The original Goodhand boiler was suffering from very bad scaling under the firehole door due to the small water space, and could not be accessed to remove it. The decision was therefore made to replace the boiler with one of the two Gower boilers that John had had made for the Curwens before Gower retired. A new turret was required for this, otherwise the existing pipework was retained apart from the main steam pipes to the cylinders.
8) New main steam pipes to the cylinders were fitted, of larger diameter to match the increased dry-pipe diameter of the Gower boiler, and a pitcher-Tee (i.e. a junction formed of two curved pipes back-to-back rather than at right-angles) fitted on the dry-pipe extension from the front tubeplate. From this, two pipes ran out through the smokebox side to self-aligning unions tapped into the cylinder covers.
9) Steam-operated draincocks of the Okadee pattern were designed and fitted to the cylinders.

This completed the modifications, and the engine was reassembled and filled with water to enable the balancing weigh-in to take place. Despite all the added front-end weight, it was STILL tail heavy with the engine suspended midway between the driving wheels. The two steel weights at the front were therefore cased between them and the resulting box steadily filled with molten lead until finally, just as the lead reached the top of the box, balance was achieved!

(Authors Note: It would be interesting to know whether the prototype Thompson Pacifics suffered from the same poor weight distribution!).

The overhaul was not finished until just before the Easter opening in 1970, and there had only been time for one preliminary steaming before "John of Gaunt" was thrust into action. It didn't take very long before it was apparent that there was a big problem with the Nylatron bearings on the side rods. This was a new material in those days, and although the manufacturers instructions had been followed to the letter with regard to the clearances needed, they quickly expanded and seized on the crankpins, finally bringing the engine to an embarassing halt on the Top Curve. When she was eventually returned to the shed the bushes were opened out but again they seized. After persevering for a while they were quietly abandoned and phosphor-bronze bushes reinstated!

Once the above problem had been eliminated it was very apparent that the balancing of the engine had had a significant effect on the riding quality, and the extra adhesion weight and smoother steam passages increased the haulage capacity, thus satisfying the basic tenets of the overhaul.

Apart from a few minor enhancements such as a new brake valve and Ferodo-lined brake pads, No. 751 ran in this form until the end of public operations at Stapleford in 1983. (As a matter of interest, sister loco 750 was sold in 1975 when the boiler became life-expired).

1987

John Gretton had always been forward-thinking in his approach to the operation of miniature steam railways, especially regarding the motive power. It had long been an ambition of his to have a locomotive that needed the minimum of maintenance time, but why, four years after the last fires had been dropped at Stapleford, he should suddenly decide to further this aim, remains a mystery to this day.

However, he approached Richard Coleby, who had undertaken the original rebuild in 1969, and asked him to prepare designs for another rebuild of 751 which would put into practice his ideas for the ideal 'operators engine'. This was to require the minimum of attention from the driver from the minute he started the day to the time he finished, and the minimum of maintenance during the whole of a summer season.

After approval of the proposed design Jim Wickett, Roy Kempster and Richard Coleby undertook the work on a part-time basis which initially entailed the following: -

1) Replacing the coupling and connecting rods with new American-style rods incorporating roller bearings with grease lubrication.
2) Replacing the existing crossheads and guides with a new design of 4-roller crosshead running in Hepco 'V' slide guides.
3) Replacing the existing Baker valve gear with a rotary-driven totally enclosed version of Walschaerts gear.
4) Fitting new slide valves – the originals had been heavily modified over the years to suit the vagaries of the Baker gear, and could not be retained.

On completion of this work, the chassis was returned to Stapleford where it was reunited with the boiler, together with a modified ashpan and trailing truck with stronger control springs supplied by Neil Simkins.

It was just at this time that all those involved in the project were devastated by the news that John Gretton had lost his battle with cancer. However his wife Jenny was adamant that the project should be completed, and a little while later No. 751 was ready to roll.

The story of the revival of the Stapleford Miniature Railway has been told elsewhere but "John of Gaunt" was the catalyst that set it all in motion, as the overgrown track-bed had to be cleared before any testing could be done.

At this time it was only possible to test the engine with a light trailing load, as all the stock was still in store. However the new valve gear and side rods performed satisfactorily, apart from a noticeable kicking of the reversing lever when notching up. This had been envisaged as a possibility at the design stage, due to the magnification factor of the final drive lever to the valve, but it had been decided to 'test the water' first before incorporating balanced slide valves.

During 1991 the necessary modifications were made and completed in time for the inaugural season of the FSMR. With the heavier loads now available, No. 751 completely lived up to the expectations of her late owner, and has continued to give sterling service with only occasional attention, right up to the present day.

2000

To take advantage of more up-to-date thinking on blastpipe and chimney proportions, alterations were made to the front end by sleeving-down the chimney diameter and slightly increasing the blast nozzle size. This has resulted in a small decrease in back pressure and a heightened draught, and possibly half-a-carriage increase in haulage capacity. This now ensures that 751 is more easily able to master single-handedly the heavy nine-car trains, when fully loaded, up the Stapleford Bank.

A close-up of the enclosed valve gear fitted to "John of Gaunt" after rebuilding by Richard Coleby. (Richard Coleby)

APPENDIX B: BAYDON MINIATURE RAILWAYS LTD.

(Our thanks to NGRS member John Hall-Craggs for supplying much of the information on which this section is based)

The business operating under the above title has already been mentioned briefly in the main text, but to summarise, it was formed in 1946 in order to capitalise on the availability of Curwen locomotives by extending their use to company-owned miniature lines, sited mainly at seaside locations. Details of the individual lines are given later.

J. H-C. records that the original intention was for the company to be called "*Baydon Light Railways*", until the Board of Trade warned that the use of such a name would render it liable to nationalisation with the rest of the U.K. railways!

The economic basis of operation was that profits earned by the railways during the summer season would tide the company over the winter months, most of the staff being kept on during the closed period to build and overhaul locomotives. This worked well for several years, until orders for new engines slowed down, after which it became unprofitable.

Either sensing this, or because a new job opportunity in Wales was on offer, David sold his interests in both BMR and David Curwen Ltd. to Eric Carr early in 1951. However it may be of interest to recount the subsequent history of Baydon Miniature Railways, as well as summarise details of the firm's various sites.

By the summer of 1952 it was becoming clear that relations between David Curwen Ltd, under the control of Eric Carr, and BMR, which was now being managed by Stephen Brown, were becoming strained. On 27th August of that year Harry Longford, the BMR General Manager, wrote to Stephen saying that he understood from Eric Carr that their 'tackle' (the locos and stock on the operating lines) would not be welcome at Whittonditch after the summer season ended. He proposed that on returning, the men would take their holiday entitlement and then be laid off, "*with the exception of Simmons, who whilst terribly slow, does deserve some consideration for all he has done in carrying on at Weymouth with a wholehearted interest in the firm's welfare*". He proposed that Simmons should be kept on to overhaul the locomotives pending a decision on BMR's future. Longford thought that the other men would not suffer any hardship through being made redundant, as they could return to their previous employment at Vickers and elsewhere.

This was followed by a note from Eric Carr to Stephen Brown dated 6th September requesting that BMR vacate the Whittonditch premises, and remove their Registered Address from there, not later than the 29th of that month. With the letter Mr. Carr enclosed his formal resignation as Company Secretary of BMR.

Leslie Simmons was indeed kept on for a while to rebuild two surplus engines, this work being done at Stephen Brown's farm. Most of the BMR sites were sold off to their managers-cum-drivers, but the firm not finally wound up until 1963.

Some brief notes on the individual BMR sites follow.

A view of the BMR line at Weymouth. (DWH collection)

Weymouth Miniature Railway

This was the first BMR project. There were in fact two separate sites, a 10¼"- gauge track alongside the Radipole Lake and a 7¼" - gauge line on the Channel Steamer Pier. The former ran alongside the lake starting from the Westham car park. 1,100 yards long, it included a balloon loop, a turntable (built from a searchlight base), loco shed and semaphore signals; later the large station building from Southend was relocated here. Leslie Simmons, mentioned above, managed this line.

"*Robin Hood*", Curwen's second Pacific (ref.3), was the mainstay of the motive power here. Built as Works No. 2647, it was renumbered 2001 whilst at Weymouth, where in 1953 it was joined by a pair of Atlantics. 2005 "*Black Prince*", previously at Skegness, was accompanied by 2006 "Merrie England", the latter being 'distinguished' by its cream livery, as well as the addition of streamlined fairings over the cylinders and under the running plates at the cab end. The curious name was a reference to Councillor England, BMR's liaison officer at Weymouth Council!

Leslie Simmons kept immaculate records, which showed that in 1950 for example, the line carried 100,000 passengers, taking over £5,000 in the process. It had its moments, however, including an occasion when "*Robin Hood*" had been left in gear and managed to dive off the turntable into the lake! Fortunately a favour was called in and the local army camp sent personnel and lifting gear to recover the errant loco after dark.

Simmons also recorded that problems were experienced with the crosshead guides and brasses and pins in the Baker valve gear, later replaced by cast-iron slippers and hardened pins.

After BMR ran down their operations, the line was transferred to T. R. Newton, an employee of some years standing, who bought the Pacific and 2005 along with five coaches, also ten small motor boats which BMR had built to operate as a side attraction.

The smaller line on the Pier was unsuccessful, only operating for one season due to repeated vandalism. It was worked by a GCR "*Immingham*" 4-6-0.

"Robin Hood" in service at Weymouth. The distinctive 80-ft station building was originally at Southend. (DWH collection)

Exmouth Miniature Railway

This was a short line comprising a 250-yard circuit with a station called Esplanade and a spur to the engine shed. The power here comprised another Atlantic, Works No. 1149, which became No. 2003 "*Minx*" at Exmouth after transfer from Skegness; it had originally worked at Southend. No. 2003 was preceded by the Curwen-completed Coghlan 0-4-2 No. 1750, which was not used after the Atlantic arrived and indeed for a time loaned its tender to its replacement.

The Exmouth line was managed by a Mr. Beckett, later a Mr.Minks (which probably explains the name on 2003!); the latter bought the line after BMR was wound down.

Above: 0-4-2 1750 with a remarkable chimney extension while in use at Exmouth. (B.Hillsdon collection)

Below: Atlantics 1149 and 3548 on the short-lived BMR line at Southend. Note the shorter chimney on the right hand loco (See page 97). (DWH collection)

Southend Miniature Railway

This elaborate line was situated in the Kursaal Amusement Park, and comprised a third-of-a-mile figure of eight with a large (80ft. long) station building. Opened in 1948, it was not a success as site rents were high and the Park had failed to recover its pre-war popularity. Two Atlantics, 3548 and 1149, worked here, but the line closed after three seasons, 3548 going to Swindon and 1149 initially to Skegness; the station building went to Weymouth and some of the track to Exmouth.

Skegness Miniature Railway

Another view of Atlantic 1149 at Southend, September 1950. (J.H.Meredith)

This line comprised a third-of-a-mile run, located on the sea front at Tower Esplanade. It was another busy line carrying over 100,000 passengers in a season but costs were high and on a least one occasion the line was inundated by the sea and buried under sand!

Atlantics 1149 and 2005 worked here; drivers were sent from Baydon, but after two seasons a Mr. Till took over the site, hiring the equipment from BMR.

Above: Atlantic 2005 (single dome) at Skegness. (DWH collection)

Below: the other loco at Skegness in the early 'fifties was twin-dome 1149. (I.Gotheridge collection)

Swindon (Coate Water)

A local Swindon newspaper reported that Weymouth Council gave permission for a miniature line to be built here on 2nd July 1952 – by 14th July it was in operation! The cost of construction was quoted as £100 (!) and the fare 6d. (2.5p).

In an interview with Harry Longford, General Manager of BMR, it was stated that although a longer line would be attractive, it would cost several thousand pounds for the necessary earthworks, and such a line would necessitate increasing the standard fare, which BMR was unwilling to do.

The line here was 570 yards long and operated at weekends in the summer months. The 0-4-2 1750 worked here as did Atlantic 3548.

There was also a 7¼"- gauge line in Goddard Park at Swindon for a time.

John Knightbridge joined David Curwen Ltd. in 1947 and subsequently became Works Foreman. Many years later he sent Dave Holroyde some notes on his career there, and these are interesting enough to be printed verbatim.

" Baydon (and Whittonditch from 1950) 4-4-2 locos as I remember them

(D.Curwen Ltd. – A Mr. Carr bought the business in about 1949)

Locos were always numbered to show date of completion, not necessarily when sold or used by BMR (authors note – this contradicts DC's recollection that they were dates of delivery. It must be borne in mind that these notes and "*Rule of Thumb*" were both written from memory more than fifty years after the event, so some minor discrepancies are inevitable).

Of the first two, one was sold to Bognor, one exhibited at the 1948 Model Engineering Exhibition – this was run daily on a roller bed which I had hastily run up for the show. Every 4-4-2 was tested on this when new or overhauled.

Following the success of the Weymouth railway, which was powered by the 4-6-2 from 1947, BMR decided to open tracks at Skegness, Southend and Exmouth.

Three more Atlantics were completed in 1948, two of which operated at Skegness and one at Southend. One of the Skegness locos had a single dome boiler; the Southend one had a shorter chimney than the others when I knew it – always a good engine.

The little 0-4-2 ran at Exmouth up to 1950 then at Coate Water, Swindon for a short time. When the Southend line ceased operating (1949) the loco ran at Coate Water on a somewhat longer track (1950). I drove it for the first week or two. Not renumbered up to 1951.

One more was made, it was completed by our Manager who was not a “loco man”. He gave it slightly streamlined valances and painted it cream! It wasn’t sold, so went to Weymouth to assist the Pacific. The old ex-RAF man who managed the line hated it – “Simply hideous, old boy”. He preferred his beloved Pacific.

I have no knowledge of any other 4-4-2 locos, as I left the Company in 1951 as did most of the men. “

Another (undated) letter from Mr.Knightbridge in John Hall-Craggs’ files repeats much of the above information, but adds the following :

“….. I joined the firm early in ’47, and found the locos were at the chassis stage. Boilers were obtained from T.Goodhand of Gillingham (as were ALL the boilers) and the locos finished. One went initially to a line at Hilsea (near Southsea) but shortly afterwards was returned and sold to a line at St.Helens in Lancs.

It was decided to lay a line at Weymouth, alongside the Radipole Lake, and use the second Pacific as a source of revenue. In order to get the concession to run the 10¼ line BMR had to agree to operate a 7¼ line on the pier. A GCR 4-6-0 was acquired…but had not sufficient power to pull the train. It was returned to Baydon where I enlarged the cylinders and valves.

The loco was now quite lively but the line was not popular and most weeks the track was thrown into the sea by inebriated sailors on shore leave. The line was very soon scrapped and ‘Immingham’ returned….

…. Much later the 4-6-2 was joined by an Atlantic, semi-streamlined much to the disgust of Mr. Simmonds, who managed the line, and was the senior driver.

… Towards the end of DC Ltd we took on odd turning and other work in an effort to keep going, but of course our ancient machining was not suitable for contract work.

The 1952 season I was lent to Butterells to run their line at Cleethorpes. Hard work keeping the locos in working order, but we had a good season. DID I long for a couple of Atlantics!

Upon my return DC Ltd had virtually finished and I had to get a proper job.

The Weymouth drivers were Mr. L. Simmonds (ex Wing Commander), Mr. Wiltshire and one other.

The Skegness drivers were Mr.J.,Buxton, Mr. R.Jenkins and a lad.”

Appendix C : SUMMARY OF CURRENT LOCATIONS AND STATUS

Ref.	Location	Status
1	Gt.Cockcrow Rwy, Chertsey	In Use
2	Kirkby Green LR, Lincs.	In Use
3	J.Nemeth Engineering, Glos.	Under Repair
4	Stapleford MR, Leics	In Use
5	Audley End Rwy, Essex	In Use
6	South Africa	Under Repair
7	Bickington Rwy, Devon	Under Repair
8	Private Owner, Wilts	Stored serviceable
9	South America -?-	?
10	Unknown	-
11	Cleethorpes Coast LR, Lincs	Awaiting restoration
12	Rudyard Lake Rwy, Staffs	In Use
13	Private Owner, Aberystwyth	Stored
14	Talyllyn Rwy, Gwynedd	In Use as wagon
15	Private Owner, Congleton, Cheshire	In Use

"A Shed-Full of Curwens". All seven locos in the Audley End depot were built by David (March 2007). (AER)

16	Private Owner, Surrey	Under restoration
17	Stapleford MR,Leics	In Use
18	Private Owner, Worcs.	In Use
19	Royal Victoria Rwy, Hants.	In Use
20	Royal Victoria Rwy, Hants	In Use
21	Private Owner, Herts.	Under Repair
22	Private Owner,Lincs	Stored
23	Audley End Rwy, Essex	In Use
24	Scrapped	-
25	Private Owner, Herefords	Under Repair
26	Hollycombe, Hants	In Use
27	Private Owner, Oxon.	In Use
28	Private Owner, Worcs.	Unknown
29	Forest RR, Dobwalls, Cornwall	Unknown
30	Eastleigh Lakeside Rwy, Hants	In Use
31	Downs School, Herefords.	In Use
32	Beer Heights LR, Devon	In Use
33	D.Curwen, All Cannings	Stored
34	Unknown	-
35	Audley End Rwy, Essex	In Use
36	Royal Victoria Rwy, Hants	Under Repair
37	Fairbourne Rwy, Gwynedd	In Use
38	Fairbourne Rwy, Gwynedd	In Use
39	Forest RR, Dobwalls, Cornwall	Unknown
40	Private Owner,Perths	In Use
41	Audley End Rwy, Essex	In Use
42	Audley End Rwy, Essex	On Display
43	Audley End Rwy, Essex	In Use
44	Audley End Rwy, Essex	Stored u/s
45	Audley End Rwy, Essex	In Use
46	Unknown	Unknown
47	Private Owner, Wilts	Stored serviceable

It is worth noting that almost half of the locomotives built by David Curwen are still in use, and only one is definitely known to be scrapped. Considering that their ages range from ten to sixty, this is a remarkable record.

APPENDIX E: LOCOMOTIVES DESIGNED BY DAVID CURWEN AND BUILT BY OTHERS

(N.B. Early Severn-Lamb-built locos carried plates lettered "Designed by David Curwen" (marked DDC below). After 1973 this seems to have been discontinued; David comments rather sadly in his book that he 'lost touch with the firm in later years').

This neat little 0-6-0 was David's first design for another builder, Berwyn Engineering. Designed for Longleat, it has spent most of its life on the Lappa Valley line in Cornwall, September 2007. (D.T.Rowe)

48) Berwyn Engineering 0-6-0

Built to 15-inch gauge 1967 as "MUFFIN"

Supplied new to Longleat Rwy, Wilts.
11/74 Axe & Lym Valleys Light Rwy., Combpeyne, Devon.
5/76 Lappa Valley Rwy., Cornwall, numbered '4', "Muffin".
On loan to Blenheim Palace Rwy '76, returned by 7/76.
By 5/91 renumbered '2'. Retained name "Muffin".
1991 rebuilt by N.J.Tambling.

49) Severn-Lamb "Western"-class 6-6w 'diesel'

These were somewhat similar to David Curwen's own Western 'diesels', though he bemoans the fact that as an economy measure the builder squared off the front corners between the side-glass and windscreen,

The first of five "Western"-class diesels built to David's design by Severn-Lamb Ltd was "Western Comet", seen here at its original home, the Brooklands Miniature Railway, Worthing, 1988. (B.Palmer)

thus somewhat spoiling the effect of what is generally regarded as a very elegant prototype design.

a) "WESTERN COMET"

Built to 10¼-inch gauge 1967 as 6-6wPH. Works No. SL/67 (DDC plates).

Supplied new to Brooklands MR, Worthing.
3/06 to Joe Nemeth,, Severn Beach, Glos.
2/07 to Royal Victoria Rwy, where rebuilt to 6-6wDH and re-named D1002 "Western Explorer".

b) "AYR PRINCESS"

Built to 10¼-inch gauge 1968 as 6-6wPH.Works No.SL/68 (DDC plates).

Supplied new to Ayr Min. Rwy.
Rebuilt by Severn-Lamb 1991 with Perkins diesel engine.
3/07 stored Ayrshire for proposed new line at Ballantrae.

c) "ST. ALBANS COMET"

Built to 10¼-inch gauge 1969 as 6-6wPM. Works No. SL/69 (DDC plates)

Supplied new to Verulaneum Park, St. Albans.
by -/77 J. Ayers (dlr), Southall.
by 4/79 Basildon Zoo Min. Rwy., Basildon.
c.10/86 stored
-/88 Basildon Min. Rwy, Pitsea, Essex where renamed "Western Courier"
by 7/90.

9/05 Royal Victoria Rwy, where name reverted to "St. Albans Comet".
10/07 to Wat Tyler Railway, Pitsea, Essex (on hire from FMB Engineering).

d) "LUTON COMET"

Built to 10¼-inch gauge 1970 as 6-6wPM. Works No. SL/70 (DDC plates)

Supplied new to Wardown Park Min. Rwy., Luton

Severn-Lamb Westerns were recognisable by their conspicuous front grilles as well as the square corners to the cab windows. This is "Western Courier" whilst at Basildon (September 1990). (DWH)

By 8/72 Chelmsley Wood Min. Rwy, West Mids., where renamed "Chelmsley Flyer".
c./83 Mr. Wilthrop, Maxstoke, Warwicks.
c./85 S. Camps, Tamworth, Staffs.
9/93 Peter Howard, Langley, Kent, where renamed "Western Warrior".
By 10/98 Bill Best, Bredgar, Kent.
6/01 Newby Hall Min. Rwy., Ripon, Yorks, where rebuilt to 6-6wGasM and renamed D1017 "Lady Mary Vyner".

e) "PRINCESS ANNE"

Built to 15inch gauge 1971 as 6-6wDH. Works No.SL/1971 (DDC plates)

Supplied new to Lakeside Min. Rwy, Southport.
Repaired by A Keef 2003.
c.5/06 Austin Moss, Windmill Farm, Burscough, Lancs for repair.

Above: "Luton Comet" brand new on the Severn-Lamb test track, Stratford, 1970. (J.Doyle)

Below: "Luton Comet" received the more dignified name of "Lady Mary Vyner" after transfer to the Newby Hall MR at Ripon, October 2006. (DWH)

Above: the fifth Severn-Lamb Western was scaled up to 15-inch gauge for the Lakeside MR at Southport, where it was named "Princess Anne", (October 1989). (G.Clarke)

Below: a "Pride of Westerns" at the Royal Victoria Railway, 2007. (B.Gent)

The much-travelled "Shelagh of Eskdale", seen here back home at Ravenglass, July 1988. (G.Clarke)

50) "Shelagh of Eskdale" 4-6-4DH

Built to 15inch gauge by Severn-Lamb 1969 (DDC plates), using frames built by Heathcotes Ltd.

Supplied new to Ravenglass & Eskdale Rwy.
Loaned out as follows :-

/81 - /83 Romney Hythe & Dymchurch Rwy, Kent.(*)
3/84 - 10/84 Liverpool Garden Festival
6/85 - 9/85 Britannia Park, Shipley, Derbys.
3/90 -11/90 Gateshead Garden Festival

* used on daily School Train pending arrival of Romney's own diesels.

51) Severn-Lamb 0-6-2T

a) "DOUGAL"

Built 1970 to 15" gauge, Works Plates SL/1970 (DDC)

Supplied new to Longleat Railway as No. 3 "Dougal".
11/74 to Axe & Lym Valleys Light Railway, Combepyne, Devon, where later renamed "Axe".
4/75 returned to Longleat, original name restored.
12/04 to Evesham Vale Light Railway, Evesham, Worcs.

Above: another design for Longleat but this time built by Severn-Lamb, "Dougal" remained there for thirty years before moving to Evesham Vale, where it is seen soon after arrival (April 2005) (N.Knight)

Below: a twin to "Dougal" is "Powys", built for the Rhiw Valley Light Railway. (May 2007) (DWH)

b) "POWYS"

Built 1973 to 15" gauge, Works No.SL20/73 (DDC)

Supplied new to J. Woodroffe, Rhiw Valley Light Railway, Manafon, Powys, as "Powys".

c) "ZEBEDEE"

Built 1974 to 15" gauge, Works No. SL34/74.

Supplied new to Lappa Valley Railway, St. Newlyn East, Cornwall as No. 1 "Zebedee".
Rebuilt by N.Tambling 1990 to 0-6-4T.

A modified cab distinguishes "Zebedee" from its sisters (brothers?). Seen on the Lappa Valley line, August 2005. (P.Groom)

52) Severn-Lamb Rio Grande steam-outline i/c engined 2-8-0

This Curwen design was based on the Denver & Rio Grande Class C16 2-8-0 (3ft-gauge), built by Baldwin from 1882 onwards – several survive in preservation. The Severn-Lamb version was very successful, more than two dozen examples being produced between 1971 and 1987. It was reported as still being available to special order in 1993 but no further examples have been identified; the design appears to have been effectively replaced by a somewhat similar 2-6-0 version.

A detailed account of individual locos appeared under the author's name in THE NARROW GAUGE No. 138 dated Spring 1993 (now out of print, but second-hand copies are occasionally available). A summary appears below; note that this gives details of the locos as built – several have subsequently been rebuilt and/or re-gauged.

Year	Wks. No.	Gauge	Original Customer / Engine (#)	
1971	-	10.25	Drayton Manor Park Rwy.	P
1972	17/72	14.25	Cleethorpes Min. Rwy.	G
1972	18/72	15	Zoological Gardens, Blackpool	P
1972	19/72	15	Zoological Gardens, Blackpool	P
1973	22/73	15	Tramore, Co. Waterford	P
1973	35/73	15	Leisureland, Salthill, Galway	P
1975	356/75	15	Longleat Light Rwy., Wilts.	D
1976	R8/76	15	Craigtoun Park, St. Andrews, Fife	P
1976	R9/76	15	Lambton Pleasure Park, Co. Durham	P
1976	10.5.76	9.5	Clevedon Min. Rwy., Avon	P
1977	11.6.77	15	Al Saffa Park, Dubai	D
1977	12.7.77	15	Mantaza Park, Dohar, Qatar	D
1978	14.5.78	10.25	Savile Bros. Garden Centre, Garforth	P
1978	15.5.78	14.25	Cleethorpes Min. Rwy.	G
1979	15.2.79	15	West Midlands Safari Park, Bewdley, Worcs	D
1979	17.6.79	15	Lightwater Valley, Ripon, Yorks	D
1982	-	15	Domein Hengehoef L.R.,Genk, Belgium	D
1983	22.2.83	10.25	Twycross Zoo,Leics.	P
1983	14.5.83	10.25	Westcliff Min.Rwy., Whitby, Yorks	D
1983	-	18.5	Griffith Park, Los Angeles	P
1984	1/84	15	Flamingoland, Yorks	D
1985	-	15	Naseem Gardens, Muscat, Oman	D
1986	RG.11/86	15	Paultons Park, Ower, Hants	D
1987	70.5.87	15	Built for stock, then Combe Martin Wildlife Park, Devon by 1989.	D

(#) P = petrol; D = diesel; G = Gas (propane)

The standard specification included a petrol engine (originally a Ford 1600cc unit) powering the loco through a Linde hydraulic pump and motor. From 1975 a diesel option was offered, initially a Leyland 1800cc but from 1986 a Perkins, again with hydraulic drive. The two Cleethorpes locos were unique in having their Ford petrol engines converted to run on propane; their odd gauge was apparently due to the Council employees who laid the track, measuring the gauge between rail centres rather than between the rails!

Curiously, most examples carried the same number (278) on the cabside. As a variation of the standard design, a few later ones were described as 'Mark II' versions; these were built for customers wanting to provide a "Wild West" atmosphere, the locos incorporating large 'woodburner' smokestack, square headlamp, and a more colourful livery. The Los Angeles example was probably the most garish in this last

Above: the first of what proved to be a very successful design, with two dozen built in all, was No. 1 at Drayton Manor Park. Still immaculate after 27 years service, May 1998. (S.Townsend)

Below: another standard Rio Grande, R8/76 was supplied to Craigtoun Park, St. Andrews, Fife, July 2002. (G.Clarke)

respect, being delivered with mauve boiler, red wheels, black smokebox, green domes with brass trim, brown cab and green tender!

All these locos were strongly built for hard commercial service; the frames, for example were no less than 7/8" thick, almost the same as the full-size "Flying Scotsman"! Note that only the first two had DDC plates.

53) Severn-Lamb "Modified Western"-class 4w-4PH

This was a shortened and modified version of the "Western" design, running on four-wheel bogies. Some liberties were also taken with the general body design.

a) "ROBERT"

Built to 12" gauge 1973 as 4w-4PH. Works No. SL25/73. (DDC plates)

Supplied new to Ruislip Lido Rwy, Rusilip.
1993 rebuilt by FMB Engineering as 4w-4DH with Ford diesel engine.

b) "COUNTESS DE GREY"

Built to 10¼" gauge 1973 as 4w-4PH. Works No.SL24/73. (DDC plates)

Supplied new to Newby Hall Min. Rwy., Ripon, Yorks.
1999 rebuilt to 4w-4GasH.

Severn-Lamb simplified the Western design into a shortened version with four-wheel bogies, one of which was "Countess de Grey" for Newby Hall, where it is seen in July 1994. (DWH)

The fourth "Modified Western" was "Duke of Cornwall". (DWH)

Additional locos built to same design without DDC plates:

1973	SL 21/73	10.25 "St. Annes Express"
1981	SL AF81W4	10.25 "Duke of Cornwall"

54) Outside-cylindered 2-6-0

Under construction 2007 (10¼" gauge) by Royal Victoria Rwy using DC patterns. Will be a duplicate of "Isambard Kingdom Brunel" (ref.36). As at September 2007, work was well advanced, with the frames, running gear, boiler and all castings completed. When complete, the loco will be numbered 5, painted red, and named "Peter the Private" in the same military tradition as other locally-built engines.

APPENDIX E : BOOK REVIEW

"RULE OF THUMB" – The Life Story of an Engineer.

By David Curwen. Published by Vintage Reprint Service, Lodge Wood Farm, Hawkeridge, Westbury, Wilts. BA13 4LA.

56pp A4, perfect bound, laminated colour cover, b&w and colour illustrations. ISBN 978-0-9554625-0-4. £13. 50 including post and packing.

David Curwen will be known to most readers as the doyen of miniature loco-builders in the U.K; this slim volume is his autobiography. There are two clues in the title to indicate the contents – "Rule of Thumb" underlines David's attitude to records, drawings and paperwork generally (i.e. as little as possible!) whilst "The life story of an Engineer" emphasises that there was far more to his life and career than just locomotives. In fact only about a dozen pages deal directly with this aspect of what has been a very long (94-year), active and varied career.

The book comprises some fifteen short chapters, more or less in chronological order, each devoted to some period or aspect of David's life. They cover such varied subjects as his pre-war experiences whilst apprenticed to a local garage owner, war work on Sunderland flying boats, the development of steam cars, and his one-year stint as Chief Mechanical Engineer of the fledgling Talyllyn Railway Preservation Society.

There are some fascinating glimpses into life in the inter-war period – how many people remember when radio sets had high-tension and low-tension batteries, the latter having to be taken to a dealer and recharged weekly? Or the time when many remote country houses had their own electricity generating sets?

Those of us with a passion for the minutiae of locomotive history – neat records of production and Works Numbers, for example – will look in vain for such detail; many of the eighty or more locomotives built or designed by David merit little or no mention in the book. Having been written entirely from memory, there are a few minor lapses - "Torrey Canyon" for Torry Hill" for example - but overall the book provides a splendid over-view of the life and times of a most interesting character, presented in a light-hearted and readable manner. Recommended for general reading. (Lawson Little)

APPENDIX F : Talyllyn No 5

(John Bate, who served as the Talyllyn's Chief Engineer from 1963 to 1994, has very kindly provided this detailed account of No.5's brief operational career on that railway).

"..............The idea of building this small loco was suggested by Tom Rolt, who had the Ford Model T engine that he had removed from his narrow boat "Cressy". Although the Model T had two forward speeds and one reverse in the epicyclic gearbox, for use on the boat it had been simplified by the removal of the low forward-speed gear band; it therefore had only one speed in each direction. David Curwen built the unit into a light steel frame and added a worm gear final drive mounted on one axle. The two axles were then coupled by roller chain.

It was arranged that the former low speed reverse should be the forward gear on the loco to provide more power on the rising gradient up the line. The fast forward speed was considered to be suitable for the downhill work where less power was required. In fact, if any heavy load had to be hauled down the line, the loco had to be turned on a wagon turntable at Wharf so that the lower gear could be used.

The loco was completed with a light steel superstructure. The fuel tank formed the seat for the driver and mate. The auxiliary drives from the engine were taken by light roller chains, so there was a considerable clatter of chain noise when running, and the machine was soon termed "The Lawnmower" as it sounded rather like an old Atco mower.

It was delivered on 18th October 1952 and was immediately taken for a test run up the line with a few wagons, to collect salvaged rail from the foot of the Alltwyllt incline at Nant Gwernol. I believe it made two trips on that task. It then went into service as the track gang's transport.

Tom Rolt was also very keen that the railway should serve the local community, and a regular winter service was begun on Fridays using the loco with one coach and a van. The Talyllyn van was found to be too heavy so the much lighter Corris van was used for the purpose. This was the load limit for the loco, so if any wagons had to be taken in addition a steam loco was used.

On 26th October 1952 a steam-hauled ballast train was derailed up the line and had to be abandoned by the volunteer gang. The permanent staff hauled the loco (No. 4) back to Pendre with No. 5. The weight and stiffness of a dead steam loco was too much for No. 5 and the epicyclic bands slipped and overheated. It thereafter continued to suffer from slipping bands, and as there was no-one at Tywyn who understood Model T gearboxes it had to struggle on. Other faults developed including a major oil leak from the engine that resulted in a continuous black streak between the rails between Tywyn and Bryngla s.

The last winter passenger train was worked on the Thursday before Easter 1953 and immediately afterwards the Corris van was loaded with tools and propelled up to Hendy for a gang to work there on Good Friday. I travelled on the loco on that occasion. There was so much oil smoke from the engine that the driver and I sat out on the cab sides rather than on the seat. On returning light, the loco was put away in the shed – next day the engine would not turn over and as far as I know it was never used again.

The worm gear final driver was virtually irreversible so the loco could not be pushed by hand and had to be towed by a steam loco with the wheels sliding on the rails. I therefore took out the worm axle and replaced it with a plain one; subsequently the engine was also removed. I offered the engine back to Tom Rolt but he did not want it, so it went in the next load of scrap to raise funds.

A group of members thought they could find another engine and rebuild it as a trolley for the Telephone Gang. It was taken to Manchester but nothing was done. Eventually it was rescued, a timber floor made and it returned to Tywyn on 30th June 1957 to be numbered 19 in the wagon stock. The upstanding spring mountings were a nuisance so I cut them off, and the timber buffer beams rotted away. Otherwise it remains as built. For many years it reposed at the back of the south Carriage Shed carrying a large generator (now parked in the sidings at Tywyn Wharf – L.L.).

The original estimated cost was about £80 but the eventual bill was near £200 so it proved a rather expensive failure................"

Above: Curwen-designed 'maritime masterpiece' "Southern Cross" on the lake at Stapleford Park, Leics. May 1976. (J.Doyle)

Below: 'Dickie' rests with newer shedmates at the Beer Heights Light Railway. (J. MacDougall)

IN MEMORIAM: BARBARA CURWEN (1917-2007)

Sadly, whilst this book was in preparation, David Curwen's wife Barbara passed away after a long illness. The owner of the Royal Victoria Railway, Peter Bowers, who knew the couple well, has provided information from which the following notes have been prepared.

- - - - - - - -

Barbara Curwen was born in 1917 as the daughter of Kyrle Willans (and granddaughter of Peter Willans, inventor of the central valve steam engine). Her father held important positions with both the Vulcan Foundry and the North British Loco Works, and met David Curwen when the latter was commissioned to build a number of paddle wheels for a project converting army landing craft into canal houseboats.

In the course of filling the order David met Barbara, and true love soon blossomed, to the extent that they were married at Devizes in September 1950. Barbara, who had been educated at Morton Hall Girls School in Cheshire, developed a career as an actress; after attending RADA she progressed from "weekly rep" in the North of England to parts with the West of England Theatre Company at Exmouth.

Subsequent to her marriage Barbara also auditioned for TV roles, but gave up her career to support David, the couple living initially in a cottage at Ramsbury. When David took on the post of Chief Mechanical Engineer to the Talyllyn Railway, she moved to Wales with him, acting as Guard and Ticket Collector on the line.

At the end of the 1951 season they returned to Wiltshire, buying a pair of derelict cottages near her father's house in the village of All Cannings; they were destined to spend the rest of their lives there. Barbara acted as secretary and book-keeper to David's new business, Curwen & Newbery, as well as retaining her interest in acting by putting on productions in the local village hall.

She also enjoyed meeting David's customers, the couple forming a lifelong friendship with Lord Braybooke at Audley End. They also stayed with Lord Gretton at Stapleford Hall, although Barbara was less than enamoured of the green bath water there (which was pumped from the adjacent lake!).

Unfortunately, in 2000 Barbara was diagnosed with Alzheimer's Disease, and although David cared for her at home for several years, her condition gradually deteriorated until July 2006, when she was moved to a residential care home in Littleton Panell. After a couple of falls, one of which broke her hip and pelvis, her condition worsened and she finally passed away on 9th August 2007 at the age of 90.

The photo opposite shows Barbara and David outside their cottage in happier times.

Above: David and Barbara Curwen outside their home at All Cannings. (Helen Allenby).

Below: David Curwen in his workshop at All Cannings. (Helen Allenby))

ACKNOWLEDGEMENTS

Very special thanks to my colleague Dave Holroyde, who kindly made available his extensive notes on Curwen locomotives compiled over many years whilst Miniature Lines Records Officer for the Narrow Gauge Railway Society. Without them, this monograph would never have seen the light of day.

Thanks also to those owners of Curwen locomotives who kindly responded to my requests for up-to-date information; the very few who didn't will know whom to blame for any errors!

I am also particularly grateful to Peter Bowers of the Royal Victoria Railway, who visits David Curwen regularly and was able to discuss various points with him on my behalf. Also NGRS members John Hall-Craggs for information on Baydon Miniature Railways, Brian Hillsdon for loaning his notes on the larger Curwen steam locos, Neville Knight and Neville Fields for their excellent support with photographs and information, and many other members who provided photographs, the latter acknowledged individually where possible.

Also my thanks to David Curwen himself, who together with his publisher David Edgington encouraged the Society to go ahead with this monograph, which may be regarded as a supplement to David's own biography.

Finally my thanks to my long-suffering wife Sheila who coped with my extended sessions at the keyboard or monopolising the dining-room table, as well as happily accompanying me on various fact-finding missions.

Photo reproduction quality is affected in some cases by the condition of the originals, but are included for their historical significance.

Sources of reference include: -

"History of Model & Miniature Railways" (part work)
"ABC of Miniature Railways" (Ian Allan)
"Miniature Railways Past and Present" (A.J.Lambert)
Heywood Society Journal, various issues
"Chronicles of Pendre Sidings" (John Bate)
"The Audley End Railway" (Lord Braybrooke) - (n.b. this booklet is dedicated to David Curwen)

Pacific 2647 at Weymouth in 1967. (N.Fields)